How the Codex was Found

Found

A NARRATIVE OF TWO VISITS TO SINAI

FROM MRS. LEWIS'S JOURNALS, 1892–1893

In the Shadow of Sinai

A STORY OF TRAVEL AND RESEARCH

FROM 1895 TO 1897

How the Codex was Found

A Narrative of Two Visits to Sinai
From Mrs. Lewis's Journals, 1892–1893

BY

Margaret Dunlop Gibson

In the Shadow of Sinai

A Story of Travel and Research
from 1895 to 1897

BY

Agnes Smith Lewis

THE *Alpha* PRESS
BRIGHTON • PORTLAND

*How the Codex was Found, A Narrative of Two Visits to Sinai, from Mrs Lewis's Journals,
1892–1893, by Margaret Dunlop Gibson, originally published by Macmillan & Bowes,
Cambridge, 1893; In the Shadow of Sinai, A Story of Travel and Research
from 1895 to 1897, by Agnes Smith Lewis, originally published by
Macmillan & Bowes, Cambridge, 1898.*

This one-volume edition first published 1999, reprinted 2002, in Great Britain by
THE ALPHA PRESS LTD
Box 2950
Brighton BN2 5SP

and in the United States of America by
THE ALPHA PRESS
5824 N.E. Hassalo St.
Portland, Oregon 97213-3644

British Library Cataloguing in Publication Data
A CIP catalogue record for this book is available from the British Library.

Library of Congress Cataloging-in-Publication Data
In the shadow of Sinai: stories of travel and biblical research/ Agnes Smith Lewis and
Margaret Dunlop Gibson.
p. cm.
Includes bibliographical references.
Contents: How the codex was found / by Margaret Dunlop Gibson – In the shadow of
Sinai / by Agnes Smith Lewis.
ISBN 1-898595-23-2 (pbk. : alk. paper)
1. Lewis, Agnes Smith, 1843–1926—Journeys—Egypt—Sinai, Mount.
2. Gibson, Margaret Dunlop, 1843–1920—Journeys—Egypt—Sinai, Mount.   3. Sinai,
Mount (Egypt)—Description and travel.   4. Lewis, Agnes Smith, 1843–1926—
Diaries   5. New Testament scholars—England—Diaries.   6. Bible. N. T.
Gospels. Syriac—Versions—Codex palimpsestus Sinaiticus   7. Saint Catherine
(Monastery: Mount Sinai)   I. Gibson, Margaret Dunlop, 1843–1920. How the
codex was found.   II. Lewis, Agnes, Smith, 1843–1926. In the shadow of Sinai.
BS2351.A1I5   1999   98-53888
220'.0953'1—dc21   CIP

Printed by Bookcraft, Midsomer Norton, Bath
This book is printed on acid-free paper.

CONTENTS

INTRODUCTORY NOTE TO THE NEW EDITION

Agnes Smith Lewis and Margaret Dunlop Gibson were the twin sisters of an Ayrshire solicitor. They were born in 1843, and their father's death in 1866 left them with a considerable fortune, and an inclination to travel – which they did, unchaperoned, throughout the Near East. The two sisters were quintessential Victorian characters – adventurers who carved out for themselves a reputation for religious scholarship and adventure.[1]

After some attempts at novel writing by Agnes, the two sisters took up the study of languages, especially Greek. They were both possessed of a vigorous intellect, and this lent itself to the study of foreign places. They had various adventures in Greece, visiting Greek-Orthodox monasteries and historical sites, and their experience was set down in *Glimpses of Greek Life and Scenery* (1883, also translated into Greek), which opened yet more doors on their travels.

After the death of Margaret's husband, the two moved to Cambridge and there met the Rev. Samuel Lewis. An immediate bond of friendship, reinforced by mutual interests between

---

[1] This Introduction draws heavily on *The Ladies of Castlebrae* by A. Whigham Price (Alan Sutton, 1985), which unfortunately is now out of print. I am also indebted to Nathan Schur, who has published extensively on Holy Land history, for providing relevant information, and to Professor Joseph Ginat of the University of Haifa for his interest and for locating copies of extant works by the two sisters. I would also like to express my thanks to Stefan C. Reif, Professor of Medieval Hebrew Studies and Director of the Taylor-Schechter Genizah Research Unit, Cambridge University Library, for his assistance and advice.

the three, was later supplemented by Agnes and Samuel marrying (in 1888). The newly-weds set out for a honeymoon tour of Greece, accompanied by Margaret. Returning to Cambridge, they quickly became involved in Cambridge life, all three travelling regularly overseas together. At this time the sisters commissioned the building of Castlebrae, which was to be their home together for their joint widowhood after Samuel died. They also purchased and presented the site for Westminster College in Cambridge, which allowed the College to re-establish itself in its move from London. They laid the foundation stone in May 1897, and were much involved in College affairs thereafter. The twins' portraits hang today in the College Hall.

With the death of Samuel, the sisters both looked for fresh interests that would ease the pain of widowhood. A trip to Mount Sinai, long discussed and planned when Samuel was alive, and indeed something of a childhood dream to follow in the steps of Moses and the Israelites, now came to the fore.

Their interest was heightened when one of their friends, J. Rendel Harris, discovered in 1889 a MS of *The Apology of Aristides* in the library of St Catherine's monastery, of which previously only parts had been known (Aristides was an Athenian philosopher of the second century AD). The work was published in 1891. Harris was convinced that further important manuscripts could be found in the monastery library, and the sisters decided to look for them. Harris taught them the rudiments of photography, and designed a special stand for photographing of manuscripts. Agnes Lewis further studied Aramaic grammar and Estrangello (a script used in early Syriac texts), which was in wide use before modern Greek was accepted also for literary purposes.

First they travelled to Cairo, where they organized their caravan for the onward trip and enlisted the help of the local Greek Archbishop, who was also in charge of the Mount Sinai monastery. Early in February 1892 they arrived at the monastery and commenced their work in the library. They were well received, and their knowledge of Greek endeared them to the monks. Their exhaustive preparations now proved their value and they discovered most of the text of the hitherto unknown Syriac version of the Four Gospels, in a fourth-century palimpsest (this is an older text on parchment, still visible to sharp eyes under a newer one). Previous scholars had not noticed the older text.

The sisters photographed the text, but on their return to England it was found that much of it could not be deciphered. Therefore a second, much larger expedition was sent out the following year. Three scholars and their wives joined the twins for several months' work in the monastery. The team was headed by Professor Bensly, who died soon after their return. His wife lost her eyesight, but wrote an interesting account of their trip in braille.[2] But the really important story was told by the twins, in the two books[3] which make up the text of the present volume. In 1894 Cambridge University published the text of the Four Syriac Gospels.[4]

The two sisters continued to be active in related fields in Sinai and Egypt. They visited the Sinai Monastery four more times and continued to look for additional manuscripts. Although they

[2] Mrs R.L. Bensly, *Our Journey to Sinai*, London, 1896.

[3] *How the Codex was Found, a narrative of two visits to Sinai from Mrs. Lewis's Journals, 1892–1893*, was published in 1893. It was written up by Margaret from the journal and diaries of Agnes. However, an uncompleted manuscript in Westminster College Library reveals that Agnes may have originally begun the book herself, but that her time-consuming work on the Codex itself precluded her from continuing the project. Whigham-Price (see footnote 1) details the true story behind the actual discovery of the Codex – a story that is related neither in the book itself nor in Agnes's uncompleted draft manuscript referred to above.

In the Shadow of Sinai: a story of travel and research from 1895 to 1897, was written in 1897 and comprises an account of their various visits to Sinai. There is the occasional overlap between the two books, but of all the books written by the twin sisters, the two that comprise the present volume were at the time the most popular, and indeed the most readable, of their travel and discovery narratives.

[4] *The Four Gospels in Syriac*, transcribed from the Sinaitic Palimpsest, Cambridge, 1894.

did not discover anything further of great import, they did prepare detailed lists of the manuscripts to be found there, which helped later scholars in their work. Few if any travellers had as close a relationship with the monks as they, and the assistance they received is documented in these two travelogues. Later, Cambridge University published a list of the Arabic and Syriac manuscripts found at the monastery. Their work was widely acknowledged and they received honorary doctorates from the universities of St Andrews and Dublin.

On one of her trips to Cairo, Agnes Lewis was offered a manuscript of the Book of Maccabees, which her experienced eye had seen before in the Sinai library. She demanded legal action against the antiquarian, but was not successful.

At a later stage in their travels the twins obtained a page from the Book of Ben Sira – the first text from the Apocrypha to be discovered in the original Hebrew. But the most important – and least known – of their achievements was to direct Solomon Schechter of Cambridge University to the synagogue named for Ezra the Scribe in Fustat, where he came upon the famous Genizah. Its approximately 220,000 manuscripts have done more than all other sources (until the opening of the Firkovich collection) to help clarify the medieval history of Judaism.

In later life, between their travels, they entertained widely (with a reputation for being somewhat eccentric hostesses), spoke at learned societies, and wrote yet more books. Castlebrae became the centre of a social, intellectual and religious circle. Their embracing of religious scholarship was already nascent in the form of a predilection toward Semitic languages and a keenness to learn quickly and expertly other languages and writing. But primarily it resulted from deep religious conviction which was reinforced by reading the Bible devotionally in original tongues.

An important aspect of their success was that they were women who chose to live and work in an environment that was essentially hostile to the female sex in its attempts to gain a foothold in academia. Their lives and personalities had a liberating effect on women as a whole, and especially on young women scholars who visited in Cambridge.

Their perseverance (and luck), coupled with all the very best qualities of the Victorian Discoverer, gained them a richly deserved international respect for their biblical scholarship.

For the Scholar, this book is a welcome reprint[5] of two worthy texts, with their focus on the vagaries and excitement of historical, biblical research. For the Traveller, it is a record of the hardships and rewards of travel one hundred years ago. And for the Christian, there lies within the discovery of a very remarkable variant of the reported spoken word of Jesus Christ (Matthew xii: 36). As the sisters point out, "the witness of this text to itself is so striking that every scholar and every thoughtful man or woman to whom we have told it considers it important". Irrespective of faith, the message of this finding – that the *ideal* is not to engage in a passive abstention from evil, but rather to promote active kindness to our fellow men and women – is universal and humanistic. And as the sisters themselves point out at the end of this book: No more precious lesson than this has been found under the Shadow of Sinai.

Anthony Grahame

---

[5] Some minor changes to the text have been made to this one-volume edition in places where the original text contained Greek, Hebrew and Arabic (though some of the Greek is retained). The original books also included a number of photo illustrations; unfortunately, due to the poor quality of the originals, it has not been possible to incorporate these in the present edition. (*The Ladies of Castlebrae* [see footnote 1] has a particularly good selection of photos of the twins and the places and people they came into contact with.) The cover picture is a line drawing by Mrs D. Gibson, from *In the Shadow of Sinai*.

How the Codex was Found

A Narrative of Two Visits to Sinai
From Mrs. Lewis's Journals, 1892–1893

BY

Margaret Dunlop Gibson

CHAPTER I

THE FIRST VISIT TO SINAI

THE NARRATIVE of these two journeys is of special interest, because the first one, that made by my twin sister, Mrs. Lewis, and myself, in 1892, led to the discovery of an early and important codex of ancient Syriac gospels, as well as of three other valuable codices of later date; while that made by us this year in company with the late Professor Bensly and his wife, Mr. J. Rendel Harris, and Mr. and Mrs. F. C. Burkitt was undertaken for the purpose of deciphering the precious manuscript to which we have alluded.

Abler pens than mine will write about these Syriac gospels. It is impossible to predict what may be their future influence on theological thought; yet on me devolves the task of telling how the codex was found, having been, to use a scriptural expression, an eye-witness of these things from the beginning. Many inaccurate statements have been made by too hasty writers in our public prints, and it has occurred to me that the best means of removing misconceptions on the subject is to reprint my sister's journal of our trips to Sinai in 1892 and 1893, from the columns of the *Presbyterian Churchman*, which has welcomed the narratives of all her journeys for the last twelve years. A contemporary account written from day to day by the chief actor in any event, however artless and unrestrained in style, is of the first quality in historical value. I will therefore confine myself to filling up the

3

gap between the two journals and giving a short account of the convent of St. Catherine. Suffice it to say here that only three persons were present when the codex was found in February 1892, viz., Father Galaktéon, the monk-librarian of the convent, Mrs. Lewis, and myself. Two of this trio being completely innocent of Syriac, my sister was practically alone in discovering the codex, though she will never cease to feel grateful to the distinguished scholar who had put her on the track of it.

For many years my sister had been desirous of going to Mount Sinai, simply on account of its hallowed associations, and because my dear husband had visited it before our marriage on his way to Petra. I cannot say that the library or its MSS were chiefly in her thoughts, but the publication by Mr. J. Rendel Harris in the winter of 1891 of the Apology of Aristides, which he had found there two years previously, renewed her eagerness, and Mr. Harris himself did more than encourage her by vigorously expressing the opinion that something more might be got out of the early Estrangelo MSS, in the convent library, and by his suggestion that she should allow him to teach her the art of photographing such MSS. He even designed a MS stand for us, in order to avoid the difficulties he had himself experienced; but while we went to Sinai, he went to Jerusalem and Athos. We had a secret consciousness before starting that we were otherwise not badly equipped for the task of finding something valuable, if there were anything valuable to be found.

We had many years previously studied ancient Greek with the modern pronunciation (for which idea, it need hardly be said, we were indebted to our genial friend, Professor John Stuart Blackie), and whilst travelling through Greece we had found our pronunciation invaluable, and had acquired some fluency in the modern idiom. We had been lodged on several occasions in Greek monasteries, and found intercourse with their inmates both pleasant and amusing; we had also occasionally had instructive interviews with dignitaries of the Greek Church, so that we anticipated no difficulty in making friends with the custodians of the library. My sister's book, too, "Glimpses of Greek Life and Scenery," published by Messrs. Hurst and Blackett in 1883, and translated into Greek by Dr. I. Perbanoglos, had won for her the reputation of being a Philhellene among a people who, whatever may be their faults, can never be accused of want of gratitude, as they have shown to my sister in many unexpected ways.

After having studied Arabic and then Hebrew for some years, Mrs. Lewis had not found Syriac at all difficult, and had been instructed in it by the Rev. R. H. Kennett of Queen's College. Mr. Kennett has not yet visited the Highlands, so can hardly be credited with the gift of second sight, yet it is a fact that he said to her one day shortly before she left for Sinai, "Mrs. Lewis, you will be editing a Syriac book one of these days." Little did either of them think what book it was to be.

Without further preface, I will now proceed to introduce Mrs. Lewis's diary for 1892.

I

Towards the end of 1891 my sister, Mrs. James Y. Gibson, and I resolved to carry out our long-cherished plan of visiting the scene of one of the most astonishing miracles recorded in Bible history—a miracle which has hitherto baffled the most determined opponents of the supernatural in history to explain away; the passage of the Israelites through the desert of Arabia, and the spot where a still more impressive event occurred, the secluded mountain-top where the Deity first revealed Himself to mankind as a whole, not simply to the few chosen ones whom He had, from time to time, consecrated to be the exponents of His will to their fellow-men.

Our intentions soon became known to a few of our

Cambridge friends, and we were almost overwhelmed by offers of kindly help and suggestions as to how our visit might be made useful. Mr. Rendel Harris, who visited the Convent of St. Catherine in 1889, and there made the happy discovery of the Apology of Aristides, not only insisted on teaching us photography, but lent us his own camera, and accepted with Christian resignation all the little injuries we did to it. As he reported the existence in the convent of some hitherto unpublished Syriac MSS, I began to study the grammar with the help of the accomplished young Syriac Lecturer of Queens' College, whilst another equally enthusiastic scholar, Mr. F. C. Burkitt, was kind enough to teach me how to copy the ancient Estrangelo alphabet.

The Regius Professor of Divinity asked us to collate two tenth-century MSS of the Septuagint, and the Professor of Geology to bring him a specimen of what is called "granite graphites," a variety where the hornblende has so disintegrated itself from the rest of the stone as, when polished, to present a surface suggestive of being written over in Arabic characters. Sceptics pretend that Moses deceived the children of Israel by showing them a bit of this as the Tables of the Law but of course this is pure nonsense, for a rock that is common to the whole district of Horeb must have been quite familiar to the Hebrews. So our journey promised to be none the less interesting because we expected to make some scientific profit out of it, and we could afford to laugh at the prediction that, being women, we might possibly be refused admission into a Greek convent. Our only fear was that, being such utter novices in photography, and having got our own camera only two days before we started, we might be quite incapable of doing justice to a unique opportunity.

II

The most impressive sight we saw in Cairo were the royal mummies, which are exhibited in their gorgeously painted coffins, under glass, in the museum. Whatever may be said in the way of discrediting the histories narrated in the Old Testament, it must henceforth be impossible for the most hardened sceptic to deny that the Pharaohs, at least, have existed. The features of Rameses the Great★ are somewhat shrunk in the six years since his body was unswathed, but there are others who look almost like life, notably, Sethi I, his equally great father. It is no exaggeration to say that for days after we looked on that tranquil, good-natured, dark face, we have seen at least a dozen negroes in the street who are exceedingly like him. The very flesh, and the very expression of a man who lived 3000 years ago are thus vividly before us. We spent much time in the American schools, listening to the children's lessons, both English and Arabic. But as our object in coming to Egypt was to prepare for a trip to Sinai, we first engaged a dragoman named Hanna under Dr. Watson's kind advice, and then sought, through other friends, an introduction to the chief dignitaries of the Greek Church, who have the pastoral care of the monks in St. Catherine's Convent. The Rev. Nasr Odeh, Bishop Blyth's Syrian Missionary to the Cairene Jews, was kind enough to show us his own schools, and then to conduct us to the dwelling of the Patriarch. The Patriarch himself was absent in Alexandria, but we were received by his Vicar, Ignatius, Metropolitan of Libya, with whom we had half-an-hour's conversation in his own tongue. He was extremely gracious, but said that we ought to have addressed ourselves to the Archbishop of Mount Sinai. For this prelate he gave us his visiting-card, and we found him at the

★ The Pharaoh whose daughter, it is supposed, found Moses.

convent, where our dragoman had already hired the camels which were to convey us across the desert. The Archbishop gave us a most kind reception, especially after he had read a letter to the monks written for us by the Vice-Chancellor of Cambridge University, and remarked its interesting seal, viz. the open Bible in the centre of a cross guarded by lions. He was surprised to learn that we had a printed catalogue of the Greek MSS in Sinai, and good-naturedly took it into his head that our object in going there was not only to make some collations of the Septuagint codices, but to further a plan by which the English might be persuaded to pronounce Greek correctly. "We are a poor little nation," he said, "but our language is great, and we are striving to purify it, so that now there is nothing vulgar about it." Both the Metropolitan of Libya and the Archbishop gave us their blessing at parting, wishing us immortality in this world and in the world to come. The latter promised to write to the monks and ask them to give us every facility for our researches in the library—he even promised us immunity from the khamseen winds!

Dr. Watson has nineteen students in his theological class, and of these nine were to be licensed as preachers on the 3rd of February following, and then sent to work amongst the villages of the Delta. We sat in his lecture-room for two hours, listening to a discussion on the tenth chapter of Romans; and on our last Sunday in Cairo he preached an eloquent sermon to them from the text, "Who is sufficient for these things?"

The railways are very much better managed than they were in 1886. When we arrived at Suez we were much surprised to find that a perfectly new town, named Port Tewfik, had sprung up at the mouth of the canal. We were told that the French engineer carried the canal away from Suez because the governor of that ancient town was pursuing a dog-in-the-manger policy. Suez is therefore dwindling, whilst her young rival thrives. This is surely a warning to ourselves to be careful in choosing our

municipal officers, and also to make our old institutions accom-
modate themselves to the wants of the age.

Some of the rulers of this country, British and native, with
whom we had the honour of conversing, say that the spring of
its wealth has astonished them, and there there is no limit to the
blessings which a decent government can bestow. We were
delighted to observe the look of thorough contentment in the
faces of the natives, so different from the scowls we sometimes
got in 1886, and altogether different from the resigned expression of the Algerians, to whom the French have shown
themselves very hard taskmasters.

III

On Thursday, January 28th, we crossed the Gulf of Suez in a
sailing-boat, and landed on the shores of Asia to find that we
must wait two hours for the arrival of our camels, who had to
cross the canal and pass through a troublesome Custom-house
by a pontoon bridge higher up. We amused ourselves during
luncheon with the antics of some baggage camels, each of
which had a front leg tied up to prevent its wandering. Some
hopped about on three legs, whilst others walked on two hind
feet and two front knees. One got a good beating on its long
neck from its angry master, and filled the air with the thunder
of its growls.

The sheikh, who had been presented to us on the previous
evening, appeared at half-past one with three dromedaries. He
was a mild-looking young man (for the office is hereditary),
nearly blind of both eyes, who showed his appreciation of the
situation by saying to Hanna, "The ladies command you, and
you command us." The feat of mounting having been successfully accomplished, we started across a desolate plain of sand,
following a beaten track which is constantly being effaced by the

wind-blown sand, and, like other desert routes, is sometimes only to be discerned by the help of a tiny pile of stones, placed there by the Bedaween. At four o'clock we reached a patch of palm-trees and gardens fenced by low mud walls, clustering round the brackish wells of Ain Mousa, the spot where Miriam is supposed to have begun her song of triumph. As we gazed on the interminable succession of low, sandy ridges to our left, we could not help thinking that the host of Israel had some excuse for grumbling at a leader who was taking them where no food and no water could be seen.

The Pillar of Cloud was indeed there, moving along the very path we were traversing; but it must have been as hard for them to believe in its Almighty grace as it is for us to trust in our Divine Leader when the course of this world seems going against us. He does not always explain His purposes. But the events which have made this district immortal in history are now stamped on the memory of the human race; they were one of the first lessons taught to mankind by our Creator: that He is a just God, and a God in whom we must implicitly trust.

Whilst our tents were being pitched, a man named Andreas invited us into a tiny square hut, separate from his house, spread some matting over the sandy floor, and placed some cushions on a shelf that we might rest. He also gave us a cup of Turkish coffee.

Our sleeping tent was most comfortable, but we had a wakeful night, as the wind was strong, and we feared it might blow us down. We rose at half-past six, but the Bedaween were so slow in getting the camels loaded that we did not start till a quarter to nine. Our path ran through the limitless desert, over very stony ground, where a few tufts of sapless heath or of spiky thorns enticed our camels to stop and nibble. Sometimes the ground was sprinkled with flakes of shining white quartz, suggesting manna. We lunched on a hillock at one o'clock; then rode for three hours-and-a-half over a perfectly flat plain, with now and then a glimpse of the sea to our right and of interminable sandy mounds to our left. We often crossed the tracks of flood torrents and our Bedaween guides told us that a month ago this plain was like a lake. They have had rain four times this winter, and each time several men with their camels have been washed into the sea. We reached our tents at half-past five, just as the sun was setting. They were pitched on a little stony eminence surrounded with tufts of shrubs. The place is called Wady Sadur. The wind blew fiercely on the tent, but we hoped it might change with the new moon which was to appear that night. Next morning we rose at six and at half-past seven we started on foot over a flat expanse of sand, leaving our men to pack up. At half-past eight our dragoman, Hanna, overtook us with our dromedaries, and for five hours we marched along, glad when an occasional sand hillock broke the monotony of the landscape, or a glimpse of the sea, with the blue mountains of Africa beyond it, made us content that we were on the safer side, for the hills on which we were gazing are seldom explored by Europeans. Our only diversion was an occasional attempt to read a Hebrew psalm, which though in clear large type, bobbed up and down in a way that was fatiguing to our eyes. So we had to be content with listening to the chatter of our Bedawy escort in a dialect which was only partially intelligible to us. The only times when we understood them perfectly was when they spoke to our Syrian dragoman. We also encouraged Saleem, my sister's guide, to imitate the gurgle in the camel's throat. The men themselves were an interesting study. The skin of their bare black legs is hardened by time and dirt into real hard leather, their feet are protected by the thinnest of goat-skin sandals; their clothing consists of a single flowing cotton garment, more or less white, and a black *abbaya* of goad-skin, sewn together with twine, and well patched. Their only signs of luxury are the gay silk *kafiyet* which forms part of their turbans, and the long pipe which they hand to each other by turns, lighting it with the spark from a flint. All carried the most primitive of swords, and Saleem was

11

burdened with a long gun which suggested doubts as to its ability to go off. My guide, A'agi, had made a pet of the seven-year-old camel which carried me, ornamenting its pretty brown furry neck with a shell-sewn red collar; sharing with it an occasional bit of maize bread, and pulling for it choice bits of the dry desert shrubs. At half-past twelve we dismounted, just where the ground was getting broken up into little sand hillocks, and real rock mountains were coming into view. The sheikh came up with the baggage camels whilst we were lunching, and it was here that the first dispute between us and our dragoman took place.

We had, in our contract with him, reserved to ourselves the right of choosing the resting places; and had intimated our intention of always resting on Sundays. The natural place to stop that night, after an eight hours' ride from Wady Sadur, would have been Wady Amarah, or else Ain Howarah, two hours further on. Both claim to be the site of Marah, and in neither is there now water near the surface, although Ain Howarah has a little pasturage for camels. I told Hanna we must stop for the night at one of these places, as neither of us felt quite well after our first experiences of camels and wind-shaken tents; we had told him at Cairo that eight hours a day was the utmost we could do; but that, for the camels' comfort, we were willing to ride two hours further on Sunday morning to Wady Ghurundel (Elim), where there was abundance of forage and chalky water. Hanna thereupon deliberately ordered the sheikh to go on straight with both tents and camels to Wady Ghurundel. It was a very arbitrary proceeding, but it was he who had hired the Bedaween, and our only means of bringing him to account for it was by resolving to deduct £2 from the present we intended to give him at the end of the journey. We had unfortunately contracted to pay him a stated sum for the whole trip, and an entire Sunday's rest meant that he would deduct that day's pay from the Bedaween, though he had told us in making our contract that resting days would be charged the same as travel-ling days. I also heard him tell the sheikh that we wished to stay a day at Elim, on account of our photographing, a statement which I resolved to take my own way of correcting.

Starting at two o'clock, we passed through Wady Wardan (the Valley of Roses) so called, ironically, because its surface is strewn with bits of black flint. The setting sun now showed us the first shadow of a hill that we had yet seen, and the cloud shadows on the desert are wonderful; when you see one you ride on thinking to get into it; then all at once the black thing vanishes, and re-appears further away to the right or left. It was almost dark when we passed the solitary palm-tree of Ain Howarah. We reached Wady Ghurundel at a quarter to seven, our last half-hour being done quite in the dark. This we did not consider at all safe in a country where the path can only be discerned by the foot-prints of those who have gone a few hours before us. How delighted we were to see the glimmer of our tent candles! and how pleased to dismount and wait till Hanna had unrolled our beds, and Khalil, the cook, had sent us in a cup of black coffee, prepara-tory to a good dinner extracted out of the flesh-pots of Egypt, which truly we had brought with us!

A little rain fell through the night, and the morning sun awoke our bevy of hens, turkeys, and doves, released from the durance vile of their coops, and wandering over the desert in a vain quest for worms.

A'agi asked me if we had stopped at Ghurundel to photo-graph, and I replied, "No, the first day of the week is the Lord's Day. If we were at home we should go to church, but as we cannot do so we must keep it sacred from work."

Protestant travellers who do not speak Arabic can never know how much of their influence is lost through the mis-representations of their dragoman. How much more these primitive people would respect us if we were not so often ashamed of confessing our faith!

13

Wady Ghurundel is a long valley, filled with a host of little sandy mounds, covered with a shrub like the arbor vitæ, which is much cut down for camp-fires. A few palms, and the stumps of others which have come to an untimely end, reminded us of its ancient glories when it had twelve springs of water, and three-score and ten palm-trees. The Arabs, like the Greeks and Italians, are very wasteful in the matter of their wood. A little careful culture might make the Wady Ghurundel a splendid oasis. But it is no man's business, though at present it is a vital question for the good of all.

We started on Monday morning at half-past seven on foot, Saleem accompanying us to show us the path. I made him thoroughly understand that we had come to this country to see the way by which Neby Mousa led the Israelites; and that we consider it a figure of how God leads us along the hard path of our earthly life. I told him also why we rested on Sunday, because God told Neby Mousa we were to do so, from the top of Sinai, but that the day was changed because on the first day of the week our Lord the Messiah rose from the dead, with the promise that we too shall rise to be with him in heaven. To all this Saleem assented. The path led all day betwixt limestone hills. We passed through Wady Useit (the rival Elim) with its few plundered palm trees, and soon, saw a heap of stones marking the grave of a mare whose owner spurred her to death. Each one of our guides kicked some sand on it with his bare feet, and spat, to show his abhorrence of the deed. We lunched under two palm-trees in Wady Ethal, and photographed them; we also administered a quinine pill to A'agi, who had been unable to eat breakfast. A stranger came and ate with the other men, helping himself freely from their pots.

It had rained on the previous day in Wady Tayibeh, for there was a little rill, whose water, like all in this limestone region, had become bitter. We reached the sea-shore at half-past four, and here Hanna's camel had a fight with its master, who tugged and jerked at the rope round its nose. The rocks here are very beautiful, showing alternate layers of yellow and red sandstone.

We reached our tents at half-past five.

IV

Next morning (Feb. 2nd) we had a long ride along the sea-shore, and at one time had to dismount and cross a ridge of limestone rocks where the camels could barely find a footing. The white cliffs were very fantastic, and across the blue waters is the fine mountain outline of the African shore. At noon we turned up the Wady Shellal and lunched beneath a cliff. In the afternoon we passed several Arab caravans, the leaders of which greeted our guides, all being of the same tribe, with great effusion. They would first call out "Salaam," touching their foreheads and breasts, then approaching they took each other's hands, and laying their cheeks together made a sound like kissing, but without their lips actually touching. They then said, "Rahmet Allahi wa barakathu ma'ak!"—"The mercy of God and His blessing be with you!" The cliffs became very fantastic; they were composed of a black rock with red sandstone, surmounted by pink granite peaks. The sand was of a pink colour, and pink granite boulders were strewn about.

At half past four we found our tent pitched in Wady Buderah. This was in consequence of my having scolded Hanna in the morning, about his making us hasten on so fast; there was light enough left for me to photograph the camp.

We started at a quarter-past seven next morning and walked an hour over a rocky ridge, then rode through defiles betwixt hills of pink granite seamed with trap rocks and sandstone. At half-past eleven we stopped in Wady Mukattab, and photographed inscriptions. These have been already published and deciphered by Professor Euting. They are in an ancient

Semitic character, and are chiefly greetings to departed friends, having apparently no historical value.

We started at a quarter-past two and rode betwixt bare craggy, granite mountains into Wady Feiran, with the lofty peak of Jebel Serbal towering before us. We passed a flock of goats, the first animals we had met since leaving Suez, and observed a great variety of light-coloured stones embedded in the ground, probably brought down by the winter rains. My camel ate of a little dry heath, which grows in tufts, but he preferred a thorn with fearful nail-like spikes, and did not disdain wood! We reached our camp in Wady Feiran after the moon and stars were out, and our camels showed they could walk quickly if they liked.

Next morning we walked for half-an-hour till our camels overtook us, and stopped to photograph Hasy-el-Khattatin, a huge fallen boulder, which Arab tradition declares to have been the first rock struck by Moses. It is supposed that the Amalekites had stopped up the rills from springs in the beautiful oasis higher up the valley, so the people murmured when they saw that they could not get water without fighting for it. At eleven o'clock we reached the little oasis of El Hesweh, and were pleased to see palm-trees surrounded by gardens, well and carefully tended. The Wady then became overgrown with the torf-shrubs, from which a yellow gum exudes. Some suppose that this was the manna, but the quantity that can be furnished is infinitesimal compared to what would be required by the thousands of Israel. A little rill trickled along the sand, so we stopped beside it for lunch. A girl, closely veiled, but with lively black eyes, came to see us. She was acquainted with our escort, and her husband was one of those whom we had met in Wady Tayibeh. Her first exclamation was: "Ma feesh hareem?"—"Are these not women?" She could not grasp the idea of our going about with uncovered faces. She did not know her own age, but A'agi suggested twenty-five. She had been three years married, and had two children. I showed her my dear husband's portrait, and also coloured pictures of Cambridge Colleges, but the green turf was quite beyond her comprehension. She was much pleased at being photographed. Her clothes were very dirty, but she wore magnificent bracelets of coral and amber.

We also photographed a hill, which commands an extensive view on both sides just where there is a bend in this longest of Wadies. Here it is supposed that Moses viewed the battle with the Amalekites for access to their springs, whilst Aaron and Hur held up his hands. The mountain-sides are full of caves and niches, once the homes of Anchorites. Soon a gorgeous sight burst on our view, the great oasis of Feiran, a forest of magnificent palm-trees, in a narrow Wady, overlooked by the lofty granite peaks of Jebel Serbal, which rise sheer from one side of it. It seemed at once as if we were transported to some luxuriant spot in the heart of Africa. It is identified with the Paran or Rephidim of Exodus. For four miles we rode amongst these trees, all enclosed and tended. We spoke with several people, and observed a little cemetery right amongst the gardens. Graves here were marked simply by a small headstone and a footstone, just picked off the hillside, with no name or inscription, and perhaps a wisp of straw, which may be nibbled by any passing camel. At one place we had to dismount because torf trees, growing under the palms, would not allow of our passage. These trees gradually became less thick till we were again upon barren sand, and we passed through a narrow way betwixt steep rugged rocks into the little Wady where our tents awaited us.

Next morning we started at seven o'clock, and plucked the first flower we had seen since leaving Ain Mousa. We were photographing two "nawamees" or pre-historic houses, curious huts of unhewn stone, built without mortar, and crowned with a roof like a beehive, when we saw a distant funeral procession of Bedaween. It reached a little cemetery, and the body was laid in the ground before we could get our camera adjusted; but A'agi told us that not a single prayer was offered on such occasions, and that the business would be finished when they had found stones suitable for putting up. The Towarah Arabs do not go through any ostentatious devotions like other Mohammedans, but they have a formula which they repeat to themselves daily. It is in their salutations to each other that the Creator's name is chiefly remembered.

Hanna said that a Bedawee woman does not wish her husband to get rich, and that she will actually try little tricks to prevent his earning too much money; the reason being that she fears being supplanted in his affections.

In the afternoon we turned into Wady Djenneh, where we saw a rabbit. Our tents were pitched at the foot of the Nugb Hawa, and there to our great delight we met Dr. Gröte, an Anglo-German missionary to the Bedaween, who had been spending the three months of winter in the convent, and had made good use of the time in exploring its Greek library. He had no tent, but slept on an air bed just on the sand, and ate with his Bedawee escort. He reported that most of the Towarah are simply starving, and very thankful for the doles of bread they get from the convent. He had been trying to persuade the Archbishop to open a school for their children, and had done them a real service by getting the Egyptian Government to release them from a very unnecessary quarantine.* No epidemic could well travel from Syria over these barren sands.

Next day we climbed the pass of Nugb Hawa on foot, followed by our dromedaries. Soon the peak of Râs Sufsafeh burst on our view, and we stood on the great plain of Er-Rahah, just before the mountain which burned with fire, where the voice of God was heard in thunder by the multitude beneath.

At length the convent appeared in view, nestling in a narrow valley, surrounded by a walled garden, and overlooked on the one hand, by the cliffs of Jebel Mousa, and on the other by a

---

* This quarantine, unfortunately, is now re-imposed.

mountain named after two Greek saints, Galaktéon and Epistémé. The convent is a medley of buildings belonging to every epoch since its foundation by Justinian in the fifth century. Strongly built, low-roofed, vaulted passages lead into a court-yard, where modern rooms of mud and plaster open on to wooden galleries. The gradual degeneracy of the occupants might almost be traced in their style of building, run up to suit temporary wants. The outer wall, built as that of a fortress, is the most ancient and imposing.

Whilst our tents were being pitched beside a well of delicious water, amidst the cypresses, olives, and flowering almond trees of the garden, we were received by the Hegoumenos, or Prior, and by Galaktéon the librarian, whose eyes sparkled with sincere pleasure when he read our letter to himself from Mr. Rendel Harris. "The world is not so large after all," he exclaimed, "when we can have real friends in such distant lands."

We had a peep at the outer Library where some of the Greek books are kept; and then attended the afternoon service in the church. It lasted for two hours. There was some very fine singing, but far too many repetitions of *Hagios o Theos and Kyrie Eleison*. It was the last of their services we attended. They chant the liturgy of their church no less than eight times in the twenty-four hours, each monk being required to assist at least twice during the day and twice at night.

V

On Monday, February 8th, we worked for seven hours in the Library, beginning at 9 A.M. The manuscripts are very much scattered; some Greek ones being in the Show Library, and the Arabic partly there and partly in a little room half-way up a dark stair. The Syriac ones, and those supposed to be the most ancient, are partly in this little room, and partly in a dark closet, approached through a room almost as dark. There they repose in two closed boxes, and cannot be seen without a lighted candle. They have at different times been stored in the vaults beneath the convent for safety, when attacks were threatened from the Bedaween. They were there exposed to damp and then allowed to dry without any care. It is a wonder that the strong parchment and clearly written letters have in so many cases withstood so many adverse influences.

Galaktéon gave us every facility for photographing. He spent hours holding books open for us, or deciphering pages of the Septuagint. The fact that Englishmen should be so anxious for a correct version of the sacred writings as to have sheets of paper printed on purpose for scholars to collate them with all the extant manuscripts, filled the monks with a profound respect for our nation. The only drawback to our comfort was the bitterly cold wind, the temperature in our tents at night being below zero, and as there was no glass in the Library windows, we had some difficulty in keeping ourselves warm. This we could only do by a smart walk out of the narrow Wady, where the shadows lay so long, into the bright sunshine of the plain Er-Rahah. But who may describe the beauty of the sunsets, when tall cypresses towered from the glorious masses of white almond trees against a background of bare granite cliffs, all touched with the gold of heaven; or the moonlight in that silent Wady, so clear and strong, which made the olive boughs look like fairy lace work; and the ground beneath them, strewn as it was with fallen almond blossoms, gleaming as if snow lay on it, whilst a few upward steps out of the garden revealed a panorama of lofty cliffs, where intense silence brooded; and our thoughts went forcibly back to the time when they shook and rocked at the touch of the Divine Glory.

It was on Saturday that we climbed the mountain. Whilst preparing to start at seven in the morning, we observed from our tent door that the monks were wending their way from the cemetery chapel situated near us, where they had been holding a service, towards the convent. We said, "Good morning" to our particular friends amongst them, and at last, seeing the Hegoumenos, I deemed it courteous to go out and shake hands. He sent me a shower of holy water from the silver vessel he was carrying, and I said, "thank you." He then held up a small silver cross, telling me in Greek to adore it. I stepped back involuntarily, for I was taken by surprise. "Adore it!" exclaimed the Hegoumenos, somewhat peremptorily. A monk who stood behind him remarked, "Her form of worship is different from ours." "Adore it," said the Hegoumenos again. I saw no way out of the difficulty but that of suppressing my predilections. So I kissed the cross and said, "I adore the Saviour, who died upon a cross." Had I done otherwise, I should have thrown the poor Hegoumenos into a state of great perplexity; he would have thought me an atheist, for his intellect was not capable of understanding my notions. But it was a lesson to me never again to approach a Greek ecclesiastic when walking in procession.

A lay brother, clad in a blue frock, accompanied us as a guide. We climbed a very stony path till we reached a spring of delicious water, called "The Fountain of the Shoe-maker," because St. Stephen, a cobbler of Alexandria, once dwelt there. Arab tradition makes it the spot where Moses watered the flocks of Jethro his father-in-law. It is an interesting query where these flocks were pastured. A little rain fell and dark clouds gathered about the mountain tops, but they passed off as we reached the little "Chapel of the Bursar." Then we mounted a flight of rock-hewn steps by the old way of pilgrims, and passing under an ancient arch turned back to gaze on a magnificent prospect of bare mountains and desert valleys extending to the horizon. Then we went under another archway and came in sight of a few cypresses near the Chapel of Elijah at the foot of the peak named "Jebel Mousa," the proper name for the mountain range being Horeb in its lower, and Sinai in its upper part. Within the

Chapel is a cave, said to be that in which the prophet was fed by ravens. We gazed on the mountain top and resolved to defer climbing it till another day, and to direct our efforts towards the higher summit of the Râs Sufsafeh, which is supposed to be the Mountain of the Law. We climbed amongst magnificent cliffs, pausing now and then to get a draught of delicious water, or to pick up a fine bit of granite graphites,* till we reached the foot of the highest precipice: then began a very difficult ascent in which hands and knees had to be constantly used, and the ready help of the monk and Hanna accepted. The monk pulled sprigs of hyssop for us, and the Bedaween found pretty dendrolites for the Woodwardian Museum. Our eyes were much irritated by the dust thrown off by the ill-smelling plant called Sphaka, which it was often necessary to grasp in order to get over some boulder. At length we reached the foot of the great inaccessible rock which crowns the summit, a rock which no human foot has ever rested on, and peering over a wind-swept ledge had a magnificent view of the extensive plain of Er-Rahah beneath us. The monk, who was named Euphemios, had brought only bread and cheese for his lunch. The agility which he had displayed in climbing tempted us to think that he had the advantage of us flesh-eaters; but a glance at his sunken cheeks banished the thought. He told us that he had been fifteen years in a tailor's shop in Athens, and had come to Sinai after the death of his wife, having no children. He had often attended Dr. Kalopothakes' services, and received much instruction from them; this enabled him to understand exactly what our form of worship is. Hanna, who is a Roman Catholic, struck a false note by making a disparaging remark about Moses, having probably picked it up from some German travellers. This was no proof of his sense, for we should certainly not have employed him to bring us there had we not believed in the divine mission of Moses.

* Which was not the right thing after all.

As I knew there were three roads by which we might descend, I asked Hanna three times which of these we were on, saying we should prefer to return either by the path we had come up, or by a steeper and shorter one which led directly to the convent. Hanna, thereupon, directed Euphemios to lead us down the very longest way possible, by a path that brought us into a Wady on the side of Jebel Mousa, farthest from the convent, so that we had still five miles to walk over rough stones, in fact, to make a half circuit of Horeb at its base. I was very angry, and scolded Hanna for not consulting me. We were not consoled by being conducted through two little olive gardens belonging to the convent, in other Wadies, nor even by being shown the genuine rock (a big boulder) which Moses struck in anger. I was so tired that I could hardly walk, and long after the moon had risen I was obliged to sit down on stones to rest. We reached our tents at eight o'clock, an Arab coming out with a lamp to meet us. Our excursion had occupied eleven hours, ten of which we had spent in quick walking and climbing over the roughest of rocks and stones—so it may be imagined we lost no time in retiring to rest.

Next morning being Sunday, we were told that a lady and gentleman were about to arrive from Tôr. Tents were certainly pitched outside of the convent, just where the Wady ed-Deir opens into the plain, Er-Rahah. So in the cool of the evening we went down to pay our first call. We found two young North Germans, who said they were a party of four, and had come for the sake of sport, having sailed in a boat which brought them from Suez to Tôr in the space of four days. Their dragoman was a Polish Jew who had never been in the desert before. They had never imagined that there would be so much difficulty in getting water. We were, perhaps, too communicative in telling them about our work in the Library, and the Syriac palimpsest of 358 pages which we were photographing.

We found next morning that Galaktéon expected a visit from the whole party, and asked our leave to bring them into the room where we were working. "If they come," he said, "please go on with your work, and do not begin any conversation." To this we assented, seeing that silence is the rule in European reading-rooms. All the monks were greatly excited, because they had been told that one of the German party was a Count, a near relative of the ex-king of Greece. At length Galaktéon brought the four young men into the room where we were working; they were accompanied by their three servants, and made themselves intelligible by means of one of the party speaking ancient Greek, with the modern pronunciation, as it is now taught in Germany, and the dragoman speaking Russian to Galaktéon. When they had left I was told that the youth from Leipsic wished to work in the Library next day, and had asked particularly for the Syriac book I was transcribing and photographing. I said he might have it for a couple of hours. The Germans sent in the afternoon to ask the monks for a guide to ascend Jebel Catarina. Galaktéon shook with laughter at this proposal to start on an excursion which would require at least twelve hours of daylight, and at length flatly refused to help with it.

Next day after vainly trying to settle a dispute between the Germans and their Bedaween escort, Galaktéon conducted us to see what he believes to be the very rock struck by Moses. It is not a boulder, but a fissure in the rock of the mountainside, from which a little rill of clear cold water still flows, giving sustenance to a few olives and almonds. The place looks as if it had been rent by a blow.

As we walked back, some Bedaween came and appealed to Galaktéon to bring the Germans to reason. He has become quite a judge amongst them, having been for twenty years Bursar of the convent before he became librarian. They come to him even about their quarrels with their wives.

Later in the evening both the Bedaween and the Germans' dragoman appealed to Hanna. The truth was that the travellers had come into the desert quite without money, and the

Bedaween, having been often swindled by dragomans, invaribly insist on being paid for their camels beforehand. Hanna declined to lend anything, saying that he would not fulfil his obligations to us if he did, for he required all the money he had to take us home.

The Germans left next morning, Galaktéon having enabled them to do so by lending them £12. They had never returned our call, nor even shown us the slight civility usual in the desert of offering to carry our letters to Suez. We had been longing for news of the outer world, and especially for information as to the health of our beloved Queen, but of this they did not give us the least chance. Never again can we accept the fiction that our own countrymen are less sociable than Teutons! The monks were puzzled as to why the Count had never come with his friends into the convent. When we returned to Suez we ascertained that the existence of that young man was a deliberate fabrication.

We had by this time photographed 110 pages of the Syriac Codex, Book 16, the same in which Mr Rendel Harris found the Apology of Aristides. We had also taken the whole of a Syriac palimpsest of 358 pages, into which no eyes but our own had for centuries looked. Its leaves were mostly all glued together, and the least force used to separate them made them crumble. Some half-dozen of them we held over the steam of the kettle. The writing beneath is red, partly Syriac and partly Greek. The upper- writing of this palimpsest bears its own date, A.D 698;* it is all the lives of women saints. The under-writing must be some centuries earlier; it is Syriac Gospels, and something in Greek, not yet deciphered. A Palestinian Aramaic MS, of which we photographed four pages, is the second example of its kind known to exist—that in the Vatican Library having been hitherto considered unique. We photographed also specimens

* A closer examination shows that it is more probably A.D. 778.

25

of other volumes, and finished our remaining exposures with eighth or ninth century Arabic translations of the New Testament, which we guessed might prove interesting to our friends of the Bible Society. They show that the monks of this convent had at one time a wish to instruct the Bedaween. There has evidently been a gradual degeneracy amongst the occupants of this place.

Some of the Greek codices catalogued by Gardhausen are actually in the handwriting of priors of the convent, who corresponded in Arabic (for their letters are there), with the heads of other monastic houses. Galaktéon laments greatly that there ever was a defection of the Arabs to Islam. It seems to us, however, that this must have occurred because priests and monks had neglected the duty of instructing them in the Scriptures. During the fifteen centuries that this convent has existed, prayers have arisen from it night and day, the liturgy and the sacraments having been continually repeated. But as for being a centre of light to the population around, it might as well never have existed.

This seems to me, though I am open to correction, to be the inevitable tendency of what we call "sacramentarianism," *i.e.* attention to a ceremonial worship which leaves neither time nor energy for the instruction of the multitude.

My sister looked at it in a different light. "The lesson we may learn here," she said, "is that our ritualists are not up to the mark. The Greek Church, which they imitate, celebrates its liturgy eight times in the twenty-four hours, and insists on a fast which they cannot approach to. We must tell them about it."

The Lenten fast began on March 5th, and all the nice little conversations and occasional merriment we had had in the library ceased. We worked indeed, and the monks helped us as heretofore, but they looked sleepy, useless, and miserable. Galaktéon seemed very much puzzled as to how we could reconcile neglect of what he thought a plain duty with sincere

26

faith. I tried to set his mind at rest by writing after our names in the visitors' book: "There are diversities of administration, but the same Spirit."

The day before our departure we inspected the church, which is full of ancient and costly silver candelabra. In the apse is the shrine of St. Catherine, of white Greek marble. Beside it are two very costly shrines covered with silver and jewels, sent by the two Empresses Catherine of Russia, to hold their patron saint's remains. But the monks keep these in their original resting-place. Below this is the chapel of the Burning Bush, whose site was discovered by the Empress Helena in A.D. 530, with the help of Arab tradition. The apse has a roof of the richest and best-preserved mosaic we have ever seen. One would rather see the rock. We then inspected a little psalter, which contains all the 150 Psalms on twelve pages, faultlessly written. Galaktéon explained that the monastery had got into the habit of feeding a number of Bedaween, and must continue to do so, although it is getting very poor owing to the loss of its landed property in Roumania and Russia. On the last evening of our stay the Bursar, the Holy Deacon Nicodemus, took us round the gardens, which he called "the only consolation of the monks," and where blooming almonds and olives sheltered beds of beans and onions.

We left the convent on Tuesday morning, March 8th. We walked for an hour to the junction of Wady ed-Dayr with Wady esh-Sheikh, thus striking into a different route from that by which we had journeyed from Suez. At a quarter-past eleven we found a beautiful shady niche in a rock to take luncheon in. Here we had a tussle with Hanna, who was most unwilling to let us escape the noon-tide heat by resting until three o'clock. We had previously resisted his attempt to make us start two days later, and thus force ourselves to do the journey in six-and-a-half days instead of the usual eight-and-a-half. It was all to put an additional four pounds in his own pocket. We rode till half-past five and then walked an hour longer, for my back felt as if it were broken with jolting on a saddle which would never keep straight. We got a fright by Hanna tumbling over the back of his camel as he was dismounting. He had been in too great a hurry to wait till the camel had finished kneeling. There were fifty Bedaween encamped round our tents, and very picturesque they looked in the brilliant moonlight. We were greatly edified by listening to a furious quarrel betwixt Hanna and the Sheikh Mohammed. We learnt for certain, what we had before suspected, that an inferior animal had been supplied to me, and that Hanna had not troubled himself to inspect either dromedaries or saddles before leaving the convent.

We started at half-past six next morning and walked for an hour along Wady esh-Sheikh. Before noon my saddle became so uncomfortable that I dismounted and insisted on exchanging camels with Hanna. He had not been on my camel a few minutes when he discovered that the two horns of the saddle were not in a line with each other, and that no adjustment of packages would make the rider comfortable; so he took care never to mount that camel again.

We lunched in Wady Suleif, and I had an altercation with Hanna, who declared that the Bedaween would not allow me to keep to the easy-paced animal which I had taken from him, and which had carried him from Suez to Sinai. At half-past five we found our tents pitched in Wady Igne, though I had told Hanna that we particularly wished to make a long day of it, so as to spend the noon of next day photographing at Sarabit el-Khadim. We told him that the tents must be taken up and the camels reloaded; then we walked along in the bright moonlight, trusting that they would follow us. At length we espied an old Bedawy racing after us. He told us we were getting off the track, and that the path for a long distance would be across a mountain-ridge, over stones, where a tent could not be pitched. We agreed to encamp at the foot of this ridge; but up came Hanna and said the old Bedawy was telling lies. He persuaded us to cross the ridge in the moonlight. My sister walked the whole way, as she would not trust a camel's feet on the loose, rough stones; but I mounted wherever there was an ascent. At eight o'clock all our baggage camels passed us, both the cook and the Bedaween greeting us with *"Kwaiss kiddi!"*—"This is lovely!"

At length Hanna made them stop, and our sleeping tent was pitched with much difficulty by its cords being weighted with stones—not as usual by staves driven into the ground. After it was fixed, a string of laden camels came against a rope which was in shadow and knocked it down. The roof of the tent collapsed, Hanna being inside, and bobbed up and down as he was trying to set it up again. The Bedaween cut the scanty brush-wood for their fires and for their camels' supper, and as our dinner was cooked in the moonlight, about nine P.M., a more weird scene could hardly be imagined. Amidst all this discomfort the patient good-will of the Bedaween was remarkable.

We rose next morning at daybreak and walked down the stony, narrow valley, whose sides were dotted with bunches of pale green plants up to the hill-tops, whilst its bed sheltered plenty of the white-flowering torf, which resembles broom. When the camels came up we had to insist on my saddle being transferred to the one I preferred riding. Hanna stormed at the Bedaween, though we believed this to be the outcome of his own management; and he stormed still more when he found that the camera had been left behind. On emerging from this narrow valley our path lay across deep white sand for five hours, until we dismounted at the foot of a stony precipice. Here my sister found that her foot, which had been swollen since the day she climbed Râs Sufsafeh, had got a wound on the rough stones, and was so painful that she could not walk. This was awkward, for the descent to Sarabit el-Khadim was too steep and rugged to be altogether safe for camel-riding. Yet Hanna at first hurried on, leaving us without a guide, and it was only my shouts which brought a Bedawy to our assistance. We made my sister remount, and under the shadow of a rock, which seemed once to have been a colossal statue, we found that her heel was badly hurt. All remains of ancient grandeur are here in the very last stage of decay, statues whose outlines can only be guessed, and inscriptions being fast assimilated by wind-blown sand to the surface of their native rock. I took two photographs of the very confused and extensive ruins, and was thoroughly glad to reach our tents in the Wady Suwig.

Our tents were pitched on Saturday night in the Wady Ghurundel. They were fastened to trees, and I slept fearlessly in spite of the high winds. But after midnight I was awoke by a strong gust, and found the canvas wall beside me was being lifted from the ground, with every prospect of the pole falling on my sister's side, and we ourselves being left without shelter in the bright moonlight. I held down the rod next me as well as I could, whilst my screams awoke the Bedaween, and brought my sister to help me. The former came running at once, and for ten minutes they were tugging hard against the wind, shouting to each other and to us, whom they could not see. They at length told us we were quite secure, and we went to sleep again.

Next morning we saw the one well which now remains at Elim, a mere hole dug in the sand, where the water sometimes runs very low. In the afternoon we were cheered by the arrival of three travellers, the Rev. Dr. MacCallum, of Glasgow, and Messrs. Morrow and Small, of Philadelphia. The latter were friends of Mr. Rendel Harris, they had come on from Wady Sadur, because their tents were nearly blown, and they thought these would be safer fastened to the trees of Elim. They were the first who gave us news from Europe since we had left Suez two months previously, and we, of course, took charge of their letters. My sister was poulticing her heel daily, and these gentlemen strongly advised her not to walk with it.

The next two days were spent in a dreary journey over sandy

plains, where we suffered greatly both from heat and thirst. As
no rock, with its welcome shade, was to be expected, we insisted
on the kitchen tent being taken and pitched for us during our
mid-day rest. Even within it we became covered with wind-
blown sand. My sister rode without a shoe and several times told
me that there was something always knocking against her
wounded heel. At one time it would be the stalks of a bunch of
thorny plants which the Arabs had slung on to her camel for its
supper, at another time a water-bottle. We were at our wit's end
to get anything drinkable. Sucking at the little filter became well
nigh hopeless. Hanna being of opinion that the very dirtiest
water he could find was the thing to supply it with, and it naturally rebelled against such treatment. Khalil became very ill with
effects of the unfiltered water, which, in this limestone district,
contains a strong infusion of Epsom salts. On the night that we
encamped between Elim and Wady Sadur he had a furious
quarrel with Hanna, who threatened to deduct something from
his wages if he were unable to do the washing-up after dinner;
whereupon Khalil shouted, *"Anta Jehûda!"*—"Thou art a Jew!"
We were surprised at the expression, for the Jews are known to
be very kind to their suffering brethren, and it was passing strange
to hear the children of the bond-woman use the name of the free
woman's children as a term of reproach.

Our last encampment was betwixt Wady Sadur and Ain
Mousa. The wind blew straight on us over the sandy plains from
the sea, which was about two miles distant; it shook the tent, and
even shook my bed all night. There were no trees to fasten us
to, but the Arabs carried our tent ropes beneath the ground
before fastening them to the stakes.

Next day, at half-past ten, the Bedaween raised a shout of
triumph, almost equal to Miriam's, as the crest of a sandy ridge
brought us a fine view of the oasis of Ain Mousa, with a glimpse
of the Gulf of Suez on the horizon. They almost ran, and so did
the camels, and we were consequently well shaken before being

deposited (and photographed by my sister) beneath some stately palm trees. In vain Hanna brought me another pot of filthy, sandy water. I dashed it on the ground, and a Bedawy, seizing it up, returned in a few moments with some clear but treacherous fluid, which my little filter was graciously pleased to accept, and return as a wholesome beverage. I then negotiated with our men for the purchase of their sandals. It required a little tact, for one of them told me he would as soon part with his eyes; doubtless, because he did not wish to return barefoot to Sinai. The sandals were only a rough piece of goat-skin cut to fit the sole of the foot, and held on to it only by a projection which is passed between the first and second toes. We re-crossed to Suez the same evening in a sailing boat, and thirty-six hours after embarked for Marseilles on the Messageries steamer, *Saghlieu*, having taken a regretful farewell of our Bedawy escort, of Khalil, and even of Hanna, whose little tricks we might possibly not have found out so readily if we had not understood Arabic, or had lacked the power of getting information from the monks.

My sister suffered greatly from the injury to her heel on the way home, and this led gradually on to a serious illness. We learned to appreciate the full meaning of one of the blessings which God bestowed upon the Israelites during their forty years' wanderings in a region where the strongest English-made boots soon give way on the rough granite stones: "Thy raiment waxed not old upon thee, neither did thy foot swell these forty years." "I have led you forty years in the wilderness," said Moses. "Your clothes are not waxen old upon you, and thy shoe is not waxen old upon thy foot."

CHAPTER II

IDENTIFICATION OF THE CODEX

THE READER will see from the preceding pages that we came home laden with treasure in the shape of a thousand un-developed photographs. We were not a little nervous on passing through custom-houses, lest some over-zealous official should mistake our photographic rolls for quids of tobacco, and let in a ray of light before we could do anything to prevent it. Happily this danger did not occur, and we landed our freight in Cambridge undisturbed. We set about developing the negatives ourselves, and succeeded with them beyond what our inexperience justified. A curious circumstance deserves to be noticed. While Mrs. Lewis was photographing the palimpsest from day to day at Sinai, and I was holding the heavy volume on the stand and turning its leaves for her, a task in which Galaktéon often helped me, it happened one day that I lost my place, and so caused her to take duplicates of about thirty of its pages. As we were developing our films at home, and consulting all our friends who had any experience in the matter, one of the latter advised us strongly to send a roll or two to a professional photographer to be developed, in order that we might have a standard to work up to. We sent one roll of the palimpsest and half a roll of scenery (the roll contains 24 films). They came home much fainter than those we had developed ourselves, so faint indeed, that few of the films could be printed from, and thus about 24 pages of our palimpsest seemed irretrievably lost, and we were greatly distressed. What was our delight as we went on with our developing, to find that, owing to my mistake at Sinai, we had good duplicates of them all!

Perhaps I had better pause here, and explain to the uninitiated what a palimpsest is. In the days when papyrus had become scarce, and paper was not yet invented, the old monks used to write on vellum, *i.e.* finely-prepared skins of animals. Occasionally, especially in out-of-the-way places like Mount Sinai, vellum also became scarce, but the literary ardour of the brethren was not to be restrained by such a contemptible difficulty, so the existing writing on the already-used vellum was carefully erased and scraped with knife or pumice-stone; and when this had been done to the scribe's satisfaction, he proceeded to use it again for his immediate purpose, and to write on it something wholly different, with no regard, or less than no regard, to the probably far more valuable script that lay beneath his pen. There is nothing that does not leave its mark, however, in this serious world of ours, and it is happily possible often to see traces of the earlier or under-writing on the margins and between the lines of the later or upper-writing. Such a manuscript is called a palimpsest.

When our thousand photographs were all developed, and prints made from them, our next task, and that a very troublesome one, was to arrange them all in proper order. My sister took charge of all the Syriac films, leaving the Arabic ones to me. I own to having had very hard work with mine, having to find out in each photograph what passage of Scripture it represented, and get them all into sequence, as well as their tender negatives, in time to exhibit a codex of the four Gospels and another of four Epistles at the Ninth International Congress of Orientalists, which was held in London in September 1892. Before that time came our labours had been more than rewarded by the decipherment of a little bit of the under-writing of our precious palimpsest. It is not a little amusing now to look back, and think of how nearly several eminent Syriac scholars amongst our friends just managed to miss discovering its value. My sister, when at Sinai, was aware that this under-writing was the Gospels in ancient Syriac, at least the Synoptic gospels, for had she not seen "Evangelion," "Mathi," "Marcus," and "Luca" on its pages, and recognised similar words in the photographs as she was arranging them? I may here mention that arranging was for her a still harder task than it was for me. I could find what each of my Arabic photographs was with the help of a concordance; but she had nothing to guide her but the top lines of the pages which she had copied from the MS at Sinai, and these top lines were often blurred by the under-writing, or even altogether absent from the photographs. To go over 360 lines for each photograph could not but take up a great deal of her time, and was very trying to her patience. It required, too, the greatest care and attention to keep all that mass of material in order, and, not mix up films already printed from with those as yet strangers to the printing frame.

My sister told several of her friends of the work she was doing, and that she was reading the upper-writing, that it consisted of the lives of female saints, and that she had copied its date from the MS at Sinai, and calculated it to be A.D. 698. Closer inspection this year has convinced her that it is nearly a century later, but even this is considered surprisingly early for a palimpsest. It was natural, that, convinced as she was that she had got in her hands a fac-simile of ancient Syriac Gospels, she should long to know precisely what version it was, and what its exact value.

It was one day in July that Mr. and Mrs. F. C. Burkitt were lunching with us. After all our guests had gone but they and Miss Mary Kingsley, my sister spread out her photographs on the piano for Mr. Burkitt to look at. She told him what the upper-writing was, and that the under-writing was Syriac Gospels, which she hoped with his keen young eyes, he might be able to decipher. He became at once intensely interested, and asked if she would entrust some dozen of the photographs to him for a few days. This was on Friday, and on the following Sunday morning she received a card from Mrs. Burkitt to say that her husband was in a state of great excitement, that he had written down a portion of the palimpsest the previous night (Friday) and had been to Professor Bensly with it, and that they had discovered it to be a copy of the Cureton Syriac. It was only on the 19th of March last, on the evening before we left Sinai for the second time, that we discovered how Mrs. Burkitt, in her excitement, had not given us a perfectly correct account of the transaction. We learnt that it was the photographs themselves, and not merely a transcription from them, that Mr. Burkitt had taken to Professor Bensly. The two had deciphered the under-writing together, the older and more experienced scholar being the first to recognise the Cureton Text. What Mr. Burkitt had really written out at home was only a part of the Greek which follows it, and which is hardly yet identified.

The importance of the discovery was at once apparent. The text which Dr. Cureton found in 1842 among the MSS brought from the Nitrian desert nine years previously by Archdeacon Tattam, and deposited in the British Museum, is recognised as of the highest value to Biblical scholars and critics, as it is the earliest version made from the original. But Cureton's MS is sadly deficient. It contains—

     Matthew, from i, 1 to viii, 22.
         "   from x, 32 to iii, 25.
     Mark xvi, from 17 to 20.
     Luke ii, 48 to iii, 16.
       "   vii, 33 to xv, 21.
       "   xvii, 24 to xxiv, 44.

John i, 1 to 42.
   "   iii, 6 to vii, 37.
   "   xiv, 10 to 12, 16 to 18, 19 to 23, 26 to 29,—

St. Mark's Gospel being present only in its last four verses, and it is well known that the last twelve do not occur in the earliest Greek MSS. Here was a MS which, even from the photographs of it, one could see contained a great deal of St. Mark.

To return to our narrative. The same morning Mr. Burkitt brought a letter from Professor Bensly to himself to show us. This was a request to us to keep the matter secret till once we could get the palimpsest transcribed. We did keep it secret to some extent—at least to the extent of not publishing it, and of telling only a few friends whose advice we were in need of. Professor Bensly himself was so much excited that he forgot an engagement to dinner, and the very next day six of us had resolved to make the journey to Sinai six months later, and had communicated our resolution to each other. It seemed an instinct with us all to wish for the transcription of that manuscript. My sister and I began also to urge on Mr. Rendel Harris the desirability of his accompanying us.

Professor Bensly's new edition of the Cureton text was already advertised. With true English courage, he volunteered to cross the desert in spite of his precarious health and inexperience in camel-riding. It would be a matter of poignant sorrow to us could we think that this resolution had cost the loss of so valuable a life. He came home, alas! but to die, and the place that once knew him in Cambridge now knows him no more. But it was not the desert journey, which he went through so bravely, that caused this misfortune. It was at Rome that he afterwards caught the chill which proved so quickly fatal. The day of each man's death is fixed by Heaven, and we must bow to the will of the Almighty, who mercifully spared his loving widow and ourselves the unspeakable pain of having to bury him in the desert sand, as might so easily have happened. Now his loved remains rest among those of his relatives till the hour of the Resurrection, and it must be a consolation to those who mourn for him that his last energies were spent in so high and holy a service.

We cannot well estimate the loss which we have thus sustained for the edition of our manuscript; nor the still greater loss for the critical text of the Old Syriac version, which it was hoped Professor Bensly would edit from the two manuscripts. We may be allowed to express the wish that this important task may yet be accomplished by a British scholar.

CHAPTER III

A GREEK DESCRIPTION
OF SINAI

I TRANSLATE the following description of the Convent of St. Catherine from a Greek book entitled—"The Holy Monastery of Sinai," by Perikles Gregoriados, Professor in the Theological School of the Holy Sepulchre (Jerusalem, 1875).

"In the midst of a dry and parched wilderness there rises up before the eyes of the traveller, wearied by the heat of the sun and the barrenness of the land, a green oasis, refreshing and comforting. In the midst of an almost entire absence of human labour, in the midst of a silence like that of the dead, where there is no living creature and no social intercourse, suddenly there appears a little hearth of industry and a light cooling breeze of life. And above all, in the midst of a land in which otherwise neither the nightingale of the Muses sings the song of civilisation, nor the peaceful trumpet of the Gospel is heard teaching the salvation of the world—there, in the midst of bald mountains and steep rocks, the exiled worship of Greek letters found a home for itself ages ago, and the dove of orthodoxy, flying from the deluge of religious bigotry, built her nest in the loved tabernacles of the Lord. A handful of men, flying from the noisy world, following the mystic voice of the earthquake and the echo of old-world trumpets,* surrounded the awful Mount of God, and pitched their tents in those places where Jehovah in cloud and smoke and thunder and lightning carried out the moral education of ancient Israel, that they might

* Exodus xix, 13–19.

39

bring their earthly lives as an offering to God, carrying about with them Hellenism and Orthodoxy.

"Barren nature was amazed at their adamantine morals; the savageness of the aborigines, or of the nomade inhabitants, who were often infuriated against them, was diminished or subdued, and cringed in astonishment at their feet. Emperors honoured their virtue; conquerors were pleased with their tried prudence; popes showed their goodwill; kings and dukes scattered gifts upon them; the great Napoleon, in granting them privileges and honours, was seized by a sweet emotion and a great admiration when he found their house inhabited *'par des hommes instruits et policés au milieu des barbares du désert'*; and above all, crowds of pious and learned men sail the seas and cross the wilderness that they may be witnesses of these things, that they may behold this strange juxtaposition of things so opposite, and reverently visit the hoary monuments which have escaped the deluge of barbarism, and the overturning spade of the centuries. Such is the Monastery of Sinai.

"The sacred historical reasons for such a building existing in this place are, first, the wonderful Bush, which the Hebrew law-giver, Moses, saw burning and not consumed; and secondly, the well where the fair daughters of Jethro watered their father's flocks with trouble. Therefore both these spots were embraced in the great enclosure of Justinian, which was four-square, 245 Parisian feet in length and 204 in breadth. Within this enclosure are likewise the many small and somewhat rotten cells of the fathers, an unsymmetrical number of little chapels and temples, the historical and miraculous Ottoman mosque, the time of whose erection is not accurately known, but which must be much earlier than A.D. 1381, when we have the first recorded mention of its existence; and last, not least, the most important of all, the splendid Catholic temple, and the shabby, ill-placed, crumbling rooms which contain many biblical treasures. Of these two the Catholic temple is still in splendid condition, a proof of imperial piety and magnificence, a fine and hoary monument, admirable as a work of art, in the truest and best taste, and in particular a valuable relic of the Byzantine style in workmanship, but entirely in the midst of a dreary desert, amid gigantic masses of mountain and towering rocks, a tender shoot of fragrant rose or slender lily in a ground bearing thorns and briars. All the other parts of this temple are surpassed by the holy altar, where nature and art, where matter and spirit, rivalling one another, have produced works in which a glorious harmony is reflected, most grateful to the soul of the beholder.

"In this holy temple we must also mention the three sarcophagi of the Virgin-Martyr, of which the oldest is marble of exquisite workmanship; the other two are silver, one having been sent as a pious gift by the Empress Catherine the Great, the other being the fruit of Christian subscriptions. Yet the holy remains of the Saint are kept in the first-mentioned.

"Amongst the collections of many books, stowed away in diverse rooms, may be found not only many valuable examples in which is developed the mystery of the art of caligraphy, which flourished in an extraordinary manner before Gutenberg's inventions, but also monuments having a great and important influence, on account of their contents, on the spread of ecclesiastical philology. The study of such treasures has a double and a weighty use; for noble souls, taking refuge from time to time in this asylum of solitary meditation and tranquillity, treasured them up in this intellectual oasis of the Sinaitic desert, aided by the philosophic custom of condemning those who had broken the rigidity of monastic rules to make copies of the manuscripts.

"We are all well acquainted with the story of the sacred Codex, called the 'Sinaiticus,' which escaped shipwreck for nearly fifteen centuries, having been safely buried here till these latter days, when Constantine Tischendorf, so expert in sacred palæography, out of the vaults, as he said, brought it to the light, and succeeded in obtaining it for publication, at the Sinaitic Synod held at Cairo in 1859, from the newly-elected, but not yet consecrated, Archbishop Cyril, Constantine I having just died; he received it nominally for a time (*ad tempus*), but practically, and in truth, till it should be finally and eternally given away by the young Archbishop.★

"Of this venerable relic of so many ages, written on fine yellow vellum, the overjoyed finder prepared a splendid fac-simile edition, with the help of imperial Russian funds—an edition which he described as 'sufficient as far as possible for the learned who are curious about such relics, and worthy of the prince at whose expense it has been made.' But what a strange impression is caused by the sight of the original, of which I succeeded in seeing at Sinai only a few decayed leaves, strangely separated from the bindings of other books, and treasured here! Besides this, there are still

---

★ Donec in perpetuum datum esse (eum Codicem) Archiepiscopus collegii nomine significaret. Πρβλ. Τισχενδ. εκδ. 1862, and also *Cahiriner Verhandlungen* and *Das erreichte Ziel.*

there many important vellum MSS of the Fathers of the Church, and also writings upon paper of other learned men, among which I may mention the valuable MS of Athanasius Ypsilantes, three only out of whose twelve books were published a few years ago by the late learned Sinaite, Germanus the Aphthonides.

"In order to make an exhaustive study of all the Sinaitic books, one would require to know not only the Greek language, but also Slavonic, Syriac, Arabic, and Iberian, in each of which there are valuable manuscripts which awaken the admiration of the masters of learning. Many European students visit the convent every year, but very few of them, or rather none of our scholars, have been able till now, so far as I know, to see and investigate scientifically the Greek books, and especially to examine the various manuscripts of ancient liturgies and other ecclesiastical books; which, if they were well studied and received the attention they deserve, might throw light on many things, and fill up many blanks in our modern study of liturgiology."

A very full and scholarly catalogue of the Greek books has been made by a Russian Archimandrite named Antoninus; it remains at the convent, and is much prized by Galaktéon, who will never give out a Greek book without solemnly reading you a full and particular description of it from the said catalogue. This catalogue has never been printed. Gardhausen's catalogue, which borrows largely from it, is very bald, and gives no idea of the beauty and interesting contents of some of the magnificent martyrologies which I saw on my last visit. But of the Semitic books there has never till now been a catalogue made.

The exploit of Tischendorf seems to have made the monks so suspicious of western scholars, that they have hitherto refused permission to anyone to ransack their shelves, and I therefore felt as if I had accomplished a daring feat this year, when at Cairo I persuaded the Archbishop to let me undertake the task. It so happened that the day on which this permission was given, was my own and my sister's birthday. To return to Gregoriados:

42

"On account of the want of a proper catalogue of the library, and of a decent arrangement of the books, I cannot, unfortunately, tell anything exactly about their whole number. Therefore it is superfluous to say, that the most crying want in this holy monastery is the building of a proper library, and the making of an exact list of the books, in order that these valuable relics may not become food for moths and other abominations. I call them relics, because, besides other things, it appears that at least during the last two centuries not a few of the books have been taken away, partly through ignorance, partly through the beneficence of the monks in more recent times. Thus Lord W. Turner (*Journal*, London 1820, Vol. II, page 443), brought away from there to Europe not a few choice manuscripts, such as one of Hephæstion about 'Measures,' a Speech of Isocrates, the first three books of the 'Iliad,' 'Tragedies of Æschylus,' the 'Medea' of Euripides, the beginning of 'Hippolytus,' and other similar volumes. And these disappeared for the most part after the publication of the great Codex (the Sinaiticus) . . . The cause of their loss was the want of a proper library and a regular catalogue. Perhaps one of these two evils will be lessened by the catalogue which has been made during the last few months by the learned Archimandrite of the Russian communion, K. Antoninus, who during a visit to the convent six years ago spent whole months working among its books. The study of this library offers a profitable field, especially to those of our scholars who have devoted themselves to the study and filling up of the pages of our early history."

These remarks of Gregoriados apply to the Greek library only, but he seems to have known little about the Semitic one. We can only emphasise his remarks about the necessity of a suitable room, and we may add, suitable book-cases, in which such treasures should be housed. Gregoriados continues:

HISTORY OF THE CONVENT

"When, on the one hand, the dawn of Gospel-preaching began to chase the thick cloud of idolatry, and on the other hand, frightful storms and torrents of persecution arose, which bursting upon cities and villages troubled and frightened the faithful, then the ardent votaries of the new doctrine of the Cross, ran, some of them, into the arena of confession and martyrdom, while others, withdrawing themselves quietly from the world, fled to the deserts, seeking there for meditation and peace of mind. Of all lands Egypt was most distinguished in this respect, and the Theban deserts could see in their bosom Paul of Thebes (A.D. 250), the founder of monastic and anchorite life, and Antony the Great (261–356), who 'caused the cities to be deserted and the deserts to be populated,' as the Church sings in extolling him; on account of which, the sojourn in these places being dangerous and adventuresome, the sacred names of Sinai and Horeb, and the regions around them, drew from every direction crowds of monks, upon the Mount of God, upon the holy place of the Mystic Bush, by the well of the daughters of Jethro, and about the cave of the awful visions and ecstasies of the Tishbite. Thus the deserts of this land were truly peopled, and thousands of Christians fled into the asylum which they offered, fearing captivity and butchery at the hands of the Saracens. This is testified to, first by Dionysius of Alexandria about A.D. 205; secondly, it is clearly shown by the miraculous transportation by angels to these mountains of the body of the Virgin-Martyr Catherine (A.D. 307), and thirdly, by the visit to these parts of the Abbot Silvanus, who remained there and superintended many anchorites;* fourthly, the narrative of Ammonius the Cenobite (about A.D. 373) coming from Palestine to Sinai to worship, and the still more faithful narrative of the Eparch Neilus (A.D. 390–451), who both relate frightful massacres and atrocities by the savage tribes; and above all by the existence of ruins of old monasteries in many places, and of caves of hermits, which all testify that in truth many thousands of anchorites and other Christians had crowded to these in-hospitable regions long before the time of Justinian. The life and the conduct of these holy exiles was truly 'an exact study of death' as says Procopius of Cesaræa of the Sinaites of his day; for eschewing all evil as much as was possible to men, cultivating the tree of ascetic virtue with enthusiasm, they dwelt far from one another with humility and austerity in the mountains and caves and holes of this cheerless land, from which they came down and assembled every Lord's day in the church, where they celebrated the Divine Mysteries and feasted together, the most learned among them imparting instruction to the others. According to

---

* Tillemont, *Mémoires pour servir à l'histoire eccl.* X. p. 448. No authority is mentioned for the second proof.

tradition and to the testimony of an Arab historian, this church was built over the Holy Bush, round which the Empress-Mother, Helena, raised a tower for the protection of the monks from attack, about which nevertheless we have no other trustworthy historical information.

"But this little colony of saints in the peninsula of Sinai could not so easily find peace and security. For so early as the reign of Diocletian the barbarous tribes of Blemmua laid waste the coast towns and massacred the fathers who dwelt at Raitho (Tor), while on the same day the monks of Sinai were put to death, and everything belonging to them was destroyed without mercy. Even in later times the scourge of such attacks never ceased to trouble the weak anchorites, nor did the rocks of the holy mountain ever cease to be stained with their innocent blood, till nearly the middle of the sixth century, when a new leaf was turned in the history of the Sinai monks, and a new epoch was consecrated under the sway of one of the great Byzantine emperors.

"After the death of Justin I (518–527) the sceptre of the Byzantine kingdom was taken by his nephew Justinian, who during his long reign greatly raised the dignity of the state, and who was distinguished for unwearied activity and the greatest magnanimity. But what no less than political activity and martial successes adorns and distinguishes the name of the great Justinian among the kings of the earth is his great and wise piety about holy things, and his noble generosity in the erection of philanthropic buildings, especially of convents and churches. Procopius of Cesaræa relates that Justinian the Emperor was asked by a deputation from the monks at Sinai—since they had nothing of what they required, they who were superior to all men—nothing in the way of possessions, nor even what was necessary for their bodies, nor even anything that they could buy in a hurry—to build a church, which he dedicated to the Virgin, so that they might live there in prayer and sacrifice. He did not fear the overthrow of this church from the mountain above, but he feared it from below. For it is impossible for a man to pass the night on the top of the mountain, seeing that constant knockings and other divine noises are heard there at night, astonishing the power and wit of mankind. Before such a clear testimony of a contemporary all doubt is taken away that the present Monastery was built by the Emperor Justinian, and another testimony is to be found in the inscriptions on the beams of the Basilica (the Catholic temple) of which the one on the sixth beam says, '*For the salvation of our pious Emperor Justinian*,' and the one on the seventh, '*For the remembrance of* *the repose of our late Empress Theodora.*' A much clearer and more exact account than that of Procopius is that furnished to us about the building of the Monastery by Eutychus, Patriarch of Alexandria, who flourished in the second half of the ninth century, in the Arab chronicle attributed to him, the original of which is in the Sinai library, but most of which is embodied in Greek in the sacred history of Nektar of Crete (published in 1805) who was afterwards Patriarch of Jerusalem (1661–1669), which has attracted much attention from modern travellers. He relates that the Emperor Justinian, granting the request of the Sinaitic anchorites, commanded the Eparch of Egypt to supply the necessary funds out of the Egyptian taxes, and also himself sent a skilful superintendent of the work. This superintendent laid the foundation of the Monastery upon its present site, on account of its being the easiest spot for the purpose, and because there was water there, and one did not hear the echoes and thunderings as one does at the summit of the mountain.* Besides this, the Emperor sent to guard the monks a hundred families, and commanded a hundred more to be sent from Egypt, and appointed Doulas as their ruler. The architect was certainly Stephen, as is testified by the inscription on the thirteenth beam of the church, which runs thus: '*O Lord God, who hast revealed Thyself in this place, save and have mercy upon Thy servant Stephen, the maker of this monastery,*' etc.

"We know nothing of the history of Sinai immediately after this epoch, except that about the end of the same century the new building was visited by Antony the Martyr, who found in it many monks, among whom were three speaking four languages.

"But about the same time the birth at Mecca of Mohammed, the reformer of the Arab race, was destined to give a new turn to the history of Sinai, as a new people, till then nearly strangers were brought into close relationship with it, and carried the teaching of the new leader amongst the tribes of the Nabatæans and Saracens, and to the little guard whom Justinian had sent to protect the colony. This relationship, and the influence of Mohammed and his immediate followers, is not apparently confined to that alone, but assumes a more particular character and a more immediate contact, by means of which the Sinaites were able to survive after the destruction of so many of their companions, and to escape many

---

* The Bedaween hearing this echo, say that the spirit of Moses descends from Sinai.

storms of terrible evil. In the second year of the Hegira (A.D. 624) two Christian leaders attacked some of Mohammed's followers, and put them to flight. On hearing of this the Prophet hastened with more than three thousand warriors, gave battle to these Christian princes, and in conquering them gained his first success in arms. The Christians around the Red Sea having received quickly news of the power of the Apostle of God, ran to pay homage to him and to give their submission, whereupon the prudent Sinaites, understanding the signs of the times, went also and did homage and asked protection for their Monastery. The eloquence of these clever monks was such, that the young Arab conqueror was charmed, and he did not confine himself to showing his friendship and pleasure by word alone, but after a year he came to Sinai in person, honoured and worshipped the holy mountain, and commanded all those with him to revere that sacred place, 'where God revealed to Moses a thousand and one words.' Then the monks received him with bows and salutations, and so gratified him that he gave them the celebrated Testament as an assurance of everlasting protection.

"The Arabs of the district preserve the tradition of Mohammed's visit to Sinai, and on the summit of Jebel Mousa they show the print of his camel's foot imprinted in the porphyritic granite, and lead travellers to the place where the beloved of God sat in judgment. This document (the Testament) wrought many miracles in the hands of the clever Sinaite who obtained it. Having built an Ottoman mosque inside the monastery, he ran here and there and succeeded often in obtaining from the Moslems advantages and privileges, not only for himself, but for all the orthodox clergy and for the religious observances of our race."

ADMINISTRATION OF THE CONVENT

"The first point that attracts our attention when we try to say something about the mechanism which moves the affairs of the hoary Convent of the God-trodden mountain, is the strange phenomenon, unusual in ecclesiastical history, the existence in it of a consecrated Archbishopric. Why should a land uninhabited by man, devoid of a spiritual flock, yet have a bishop, not to say an archbishop, while time has brought changes to so many other lands, both near and far, troubling and diminishing the elect of the Church, depriving them of a name, and extinguishing them? We can account for it only by summing up all the evidence we have been able to gather, from which it appears that the seat of the bishopric in these parts was at Feiran, and this bishopric survived till the middle of the seventh century, when it was dissolved, and gave rise to the creation of a new bishopric called definitely that of Sinai. Therefore we find in later times an episcopal see in that famous monastery, always meeting with the care and favour of the Byzantines in Egypt, by command of the rulers of Constantinople; and with the removal of its centre hearth at Feiran the colonies of Christians around that place gradually ceased. Some have maintained that Justinian established a bishopric at Sinai, but even after the time of that emperor no mention is made of any bishop till after the middle of the ninth century. From the beginning of the tenth and onwards we have a continuous chain of bishops till A.D. 1510, when the throne was vacant till 1540, and again from 1547 till 1567, from which time till now there have been seventeen archbishops.

The second of these intervals is very important (1547–1567), because then the bishopric was dissolved in Egypt by the three assembled Patriarchs of Alexandria, Antioch, and Jerusalem. The reason for the dissolution of this archiepiscopal see was the constant rivalry between the Patriarchs of Alexandria and Jerusalem about their jurisdiction at Sinai, especially on the part of the Alexandrian prelates, who left no stone unturned to lay their despotic hand on the monastery and episcopate of Sinai, from which endeavour many scandals arose.

"In short, one who has gone through the history of this episcopate learns that its order and its origin in the arrangement of the eastern orthodox hierarchy was one of the most burning and important phenomena in the history of the Sinai convent. The question was raised in different ways, and never once argued according to ecclesiastical canons; it had important consequences from time to time, not only unsettling the welfare of the convent, but also throwing the whole Church into convulsions . . .

"Time and the Church have solved the problem of the Archbishop of Sinai's place in relation to the ecclesiastical hierarchy somewhat as follows:

"He is an archbishop, having a canonical descent and relation to the Patriarch of Jerusalem. It follows that the archbishop must

"1. Be consecrated by his own Patriarch (οικειου) canonically and without bribery, otherwise his consecration will be null and void.

48

"2. Remember the name of the Patriarch who consecrated him (in his prayers, no doubt).

"3. Be called Θεοφιλεστατος or Σεβασμιωτατος.

"4. Be summoned at will by the Holy Patriarch of Jerusalem.

"5. Not have the right to send pacificals or other synodical letters, nor give letters of absolution.

"And to these the Archbishop of Sinai is bound, by canonical right.

"But the Prelate of Sinai is not only an archbishop, but also abbot of the convent, and on account of that, other important conditions have to be observed:

"1. Each archbishop is elected by the synod and brotherhood of the Sinaite fathers as their abbot, as his rule is given to him by no one except the community of the monastery.

"2. He is consecrated afterwards by the Patriarch of Jerusalem simply as bishop, but the independence of the monastery in no way suffers from this relation of the archiepiscopate to the throne of the Holy City.

"3. The episcopal character of the Sinaitic prelate does not affect the monastery, for he is only abbot of it, and not bishop, as his pastoral staff is stretched out over the country alone. Therefore he has no right to sit on the throne; which stands there that no confusion may exist in things which cannot be confused, and that not even the most zealous bishop may violate the autonomy and independence of the monastery, as some have tried to do. There are in the Church most emphatic commands and decisions on this subject.

"4. From all this it appears that the archiepiscopate of Sinai has a double character, that in the prelate's appointment there must be co-operation between the convent and Jerusalem, the one electing, the other consecrating . . . If the monastery wishes to accuse him of a fault, it can only turn to the Patriarch of Jerusalem and the Palestinian synod, to whom it presented him for consecration; thus, if the worst comes to the worst, and there are cross-accusations for grave faults, and a rupture between archbishop and monastery, abbot and brotherhood, the appeal of the accusers is directed canonically to the Patriarch of Jerusalem, who can punish according to his judgment, even to the deprivation of the archbishop, but he cannot deprive the abbot of the autonomous monastery; yet canonically he would be justified in punishing the offending archbishop, also as abbot, if accused by the monastery. And no other Patriarch has any jurisdiction here.

"Strange to say, beside the Archiepiscopate and the authoritative Abbacy, there exists also another powerful force in the monastery of Sinai, the Holy Syndicate which represents in the most aristocratic way the whole Sinaitic brotherhood, has the greatest influence in its affairs, directing and bridling the possibly arbitrary conduct of the archbishop, and through him and with him regulating the mechanism of the monastery, both internal and external . . . This syndicate consists of the leaders among the monastic brethren. Its number varies, and there are Patriarchal decrees limiting it to twelve; the syndics are chosen by the archbishop and the other members, excepting those who are at the time sub-prior(?), warden (also librarian), and bursar, who are always members of this syndicate.

"This Holy Syndicate, being thus formed, is entrusted with all the administration of the monastery.

"All official documents must be countersigned by this syndicate, and be sealed with the great seal of the monastery. (This great seal is circular in shape, and in its middle is represented the bush, the mountain, and the monastery; Moses, Aaron, and St. Catherine, surrounded by the legend, ✠ *The Holy Monastery from the Great Justinian in the holy and God-trodden Mount of Sinai in the year of Christ*, 529 ✠)★

"The sub-prior has the place of abbot, as we have said, being the first in the monastery after the archbishop. He has the care of ecclesiastical order, of the good conduct of the fathers, of the entertaining of strangers, of the service and monastic education of novices, fulfilling and lightening in these things the duties of the Holy Syndicate and of the archbishop.

"The warden is entrusted with the keeping of the church in order, the care of the holy relics, etc. He holds his office for life, and must never go far from the monastery.

"The duties of the bursar are to superintend all the victuals of the monastery, submitting from time to time to the syndicate a list of what is necessary, and receiving his commands from it. He manages all the relationships of the monastery, judges all its complicated affairs, punishing and rewarding, engaging camels, guaranteeing the comfort of travellers and pilgrims, commanding the tribes of the Kaphyra, himself providing all means of transport, and in general, superintending every direct and indi-

---

★ This seal is stamped on the book from which I am translating, a gift from the Prior to myself.

rect connexion of the monastery with the Bedaween who refer to him as their leader and judge.

"Besides this private and select syndicate, in special circumstances, when general measures have to be adopted, during the journeys of the archbishop to and from the monastery, in the temporary vacancy of the throne, at the election of a new archbishop, and so forth, a general synod of all the brethren is called together, from the humblest monk to the highest archimandrite, who all sign the synodical acts, regulate and legislate, having the whole management of the monastery in their hands.

"The whole synod, besides its duties as described above, has also the duty of preserving its canonical relations towards the Orthodox Church in general and the Patriarchate of Jerusalem in particular. The Patriarchs have the care of it, and in the treaties is expressly mentioned their obligation to observe the ritual of the church, of the table and of the other monastic customs. Such are the complete abstinence from animal food in the monastery, the prohibition of private meals in the cells, of the storage of wine, and other such things; the exact performance of rites, both daily and at feast-days, according to the variety of monastic customs, upon the basis of the ritual of St. Saba as reformed by the Stoudites, no intercourse being allowed in the monastery with the outer world, nor voluntary excursions either to Egypt or within the peninsula; and the fulfilment of the duties of service towards the Altar, and the leavening of bread &c."

CHAPTER IV

ST. SYLVIA OF AQUITAINE

ALTHOUGH we were the first women who had ever worked in the convent library, we were by no means the first who have travelled to Sinai, and established friendly relations with its monks. During the reign of the Emperor Theodosius, as is supposed, *i.e.* between A.D. 385 and 388, St. Sylvia, a native of Aquitaine, undertook a pilgrimage to the holy places of the East, and has left behind her a journal, the beginning of which is unhappily lost, but which contains a very faithful description of the scenery around Sinai, nearly a century before the present convent was built. She bears witness to the fact that a community of monks had established themselves around the well of Jethro at that early period, and a few quotations from her diary will suffice to show that they were of the same kind and hospitable disposition as we found in their successors of the present day.

"We arrived at a certain place," says Sylvia, "where the mountains betwixt which we were travelling opened out into a huge, wide, and very fair valley,★ and beyond this valley there appeared the Mount of God, Sinai. The very spot where the mountains opened is joined to the place in which are the traditions of the murmuring. When we arrived at this spot the guides reminded us of it, saying: 'It is customary for those who

★ The great plain Er-Rahah.

52

come, to offer a prayer here, when the Mount of God is first seen from this place,' and this we did. The distance thence to the Mount of God is about four miles in all, through the valley, which I said was a great one. This is a very extensive valley, lying under the side of the Mount of God, which measures, as far as we could estimate by seeing, or as the people themselves said, in length about 60,000 paces, in breadth about 4000. We had to cross this valley in order to reach the mountain. This is the huge and wide valley in which the children of Israel sojourned in those days, when St. Moses ascended into the Mount of God, and was there forty days and forty nights. This is the valley in which the calf was made; the place is shown to this day, for a great stone stands fixed on the very spot. This therefore is the very same valley at the head of which is the place where St. Moses, whilst feeding the flocks of his father-in-law, was spoken to by God in the Burning Bush. And whereas our path was such that first we had to ascend the Mount of God which here appears, the ascent was better from where we had come, and from thence again we must descend to the head of the valley, that is to where the Bush★ was, because the descent from the Mountain of God was better there. It was pleasant therefore when we had seen everything we wished to see, in descending the Mount of God, to come to the place of the Bush, and thus across all the valley itself, which is lengthways, and to return with the holy men who showed us the different places that are written about in that selfsame valley, and this we did. Therefore as we were coming from that place, where on the way from Faran† we offered a prayer, the path was such that we crossed over that very valley, and thus arrived at the Mount of God. As you go round about the mountain it appears to be one, though when you get within it there are many; but the whole is called the Mount of God, especially the one on whose summit‡ is the place where the Glory of God descended, as it is written; and it is in the middle of them all; and while all these (mountains) that are in the group are more glorious than I had ever expected to see, yet the one in the middle, on which the Glory of God descended, is so much higher than all the others, that when we approached it, straightway all these mountains, which had appeared to us glorious, seemed but as little hills. It is very wonderful, and without the

★ Where the present monastery stands.
† Feiran, the ancient Rephidim.
‡ Jebel Katerina?

grace of God I do not think it could have been, that whilst the middle one is higher than all, and is specially called Sinai, that is, where the Glory of God descended, nevertheless it cannot be seen unless you come to its very root before you ascend it; and after you have accomplished your wish you will descend thence and look at it from the opposite side, which before you ascended you could not have done. But before we arrived at the Mount of God we knew this from the replies of the brethren, and when I arrived at the place I understood it clearly to be so.

"We made our entry into the mountain on a Sabbath evening, and we arrived at a certain monastery, where the monks who dwelt there received us very kindly, showing us every attention. For there is a church here with a presbytery, therefore we remained the night, that very early on the Lord's day we might begin to climb the different mountains with the presbyter and the monks who dwelt there, mountains which are ascended with infinite labour, because you do not go up them slowly and slowly like a snail, but straight up you go, as if it were a wall, and you are obliged to descend each of these mountains till you get down to the very root of that middle mountain, which is specially Sinai. And there with the help of Christ our Lord, aided by the prayers of the saints who accompanied us, I accomplished the ascent, and with great labour, for I was obliged to ascend on foot, as I could not go up in the saddle; nevertheless this labour was not felt, because the desires I had I saw fulfilled with the help of God. About the fourth hour we arrived at the summit of Sinai, that holy Mount of God where the law was given, and there is the place where the Glory of God descended on the day when the mountain smoked. And in that spot there is now a little church, because the said place, which is the summit of the mountain, is not very large. But nevertheless the church has of itself great grace. When, then, with the help of God we ascended to that summit, and arrived at the door of that church, behold, the presbyter met us, coming from his monastery, which is considered to belong to the church, a healthy old man—a monk of what is called the ascetic life here, one moreover who is worthy to be in this place. Other presbyters also came to meet us, but not all the monks who dwell here close to the mountain, that is, those who are not prevented by weakness or age. But no one dwells at the summit of the middle mountain, for there is nothing else there save only the church and the cave where St. Moses was. Having read in the very place all from the Book of Moses, and having made an offering in due order, and we having partaken of the communion, just as we were going out of the church the presbyters of the same place gave us thank-offerings, that is, gifts of apples (oranges?) which grow in the mountain itself.* For, although the hoary mountain of Sinai is all stony, and has no corn, nevertheless below, near the root of these mountains, that is, both about the one in the middle, and about those that surround it, there are little rills, and the holy monks plant young trees diligently about them, and establish little apple-gardens, or houses of prayer, and near to them monasteries, so that they gather a little fruit from the earth of the mountain itself, and these they cultivate with their own hands.

"Then, after we had communicated, and these holy men had given us ευλογιας, and we had gone out of the door of the church, then I began to request them to show us the different places; and forthwith these holy men deigned to do so, for they pointed out to us the very cave where St. Moses was when he ascended the second time into the Mount of God, that he might receive again the tablets after he had broken them on account of the people's sin, and other places, whatever we desired, or those that they knew better about they deigned to show us. Egypt also, and Palestine, and the Red Sea, and the Mare Parthenicum, which reaches to Alexandria, and also the far-away borders of the Saracens, we saw below us, as I think was hardly possible. But all these different things the holy men declared to us.

"Having then fulfilled every desire which had impelled us to ascend, we began to descend from the summit of the Mount of God and went up to another mountain,† which is joined to it, and is the place called Horeb. Here also there is a church, for this place is Horeb, where St. Elijah the prophet was, to which he fled from the face of King Ahab, where God spake to him, saying: 'What doest thou here, Elijah?' as it is written in the Book of the Kings, for here the cave where St. Elijah was hid is seen to-day before the door of the church which is there. A stone altar also is seen, which St. Elijah himself placed there to sacrifice to God, as these holy men deigned to show us. We made an oblation and a long prayer, and read a portion of the Book of Kings. This we desired very much to do always, and wherever we went we always read a portion of the Book about it.

"Having made an offering there, we went immediately to another place

---

* Just as the monks of the present day gave us occasionally gifts of dates, pomegranates, delicious quince-jelly, almonds, and date-brandy.
† Jebel Mousa.

not far from it, the presbyters and monks showing us, that is, to the place★ where St. Aaron stood with the seventy elders while St. Moses received from God the law for the children of Israel. For in that place, although it has no roof, nevertheless there is a huge rock, having a flat surface on the top, on which these holy men are said to have stood, and in the midst of it they had made an altar of stones. So we read here the very place in the Book of Moses, and repeated a psalm suitable to the spot, and having offered a prayer, we descended thence. It now began to be about the eighth hour, and we had still three miles to go before we could leave the mountain-region that we had entered the night before, but we had not to go out at the same place by which we had made our way, but as I said above, necessity was laid upon us to visit all the holy places and to see all the monasteries that were there, and thus to go out at the head of the valley which I described above, that is, which lies below the Mount of God. Therefore it was necessary for us to go out at the head of that valley, because there were in it many monasteries of holy men, and a church in the place where the bush is, the bush that is green to this day, and sends out shoots.

"We thus went down from the Mount of God, and arrived at the bush about the tenth hour. In front of the church there is a beautiful garden,† having abundance of fine water, and in this garden is the bush itself. Near to it also the place is shown where St. Moses stood when God said to him, 'Loose the latchet of thy shoe,' etc., and when we arrived at this place it was already the tenth hour, and because it was so late we could not make an offering. But prayer was made in the church, and also near the bush in the garden, and we read the very place in the Book of Moses, according to our custom. And because it was late, we supped in the garden before the bush with the holy men themselves, and we encamped there. And waking next morning very early, we begged the presbyters that an offering should be made, and this was done. The holy men began to show us the various places as we went away from the bush. They pointed out to us the place where the tents of the children of Israel were in those days, when Moses was in the mountain. They showed us also the place where the calf was made, for a great stone is fixed in that place unto this day. We also as we went saw before us the summit of the mountain that looks down over

---

★ The hill now called by the Arabs Harûn.
† The very garden in which *our* tents were pitched.

all the valley, from which place St. Moses saw the children of Israel dancing in those days when they made the calf. They showed us also a great stone in the place where St. Moses descended with Joshua, the son of Nun. Close to this stone he waxed wroth, and broke the tablets which he was carrying. They showed us also in what manner each of them had his dwelling in this valley. The foundations of these dwellings appear to this day as if they were surrounded by stone; they showed us also the place where St. Moses ordered the children of Israel to run from gate to gate, he returning to the mountain.* Then they showed us the place where the calf was burnt which Aaron had made for them, by order of Moses. Likewise they showed us the stream from which St. Moses gave to drink to the children of Israel, as it is written in Exodus. They showed us also the place where the seventy men received some of the spirit of Moses. They showed us also the place where the children of Israel lusted for food. They also pointed out to us the place which is called the Conflagration, because part of the tents were burnt there;† then the fire ceased when Moses prayed. They showed us also the place where manna and quails rained on them.

"And thus the various things (which are) written in the Books of St. Moses as having been done in this place, namely, this valley, which, as I said, lies under the Mount of God, the holy Sinai, were shown to us, which it would be enough if I wrote them all singly, because no one could retain so much, but when you read the holy Books of Moses with devotion, all things are more closely seen which were done here. For this is the valley where the Passover was celebrated when a year had passed from the departure of the children of Israel out of the land of Egypt, because in that valley the children of Israel remained some time, that is, while St. Moses ascended into the Mount of God, and descended the first and second times; and again, they remained there for some time while the Tabernacle was being made, and the various things which were shown in the Mount of God. The same day we met with some very holy monks, who on account of their age or imbecility cannot go to the Mount of God to make offerings, but who nevertheless deigned to take us into their monasteries.

"Thus having seen all the holy places which we desired, and all the places where the children of Israel passed going and coming to the Mount

* Exodus xxxii, 27.
† Numbers xi, 3.

57

of God, having seen also the holy men who dwelt there, we returned to Faran in the name of God. And we ought to give thanks to God in everything, I will not say in so many and such things as He has designed to confer upon me, an unworthy woman of no merit, that I should walk about all the places of which I was not worthy; nor can I sufficiently thank all those holy men who deigned to take my little self with a willing mind into their monasteries, and lead me about through all those places which I asked about according to the Scriptures. Many also of these holy men themselves, who dwelt in the mountain of God or round about it, deigned to accompany us to Faran, those at least who were stronger in body."

We refer those of our readers who wish to know more of St. Sylvia's diary to the story itself, in the original Latin, by J. F. Gamurrini (Rome, ex typis Vaticanis, 1888). There they will learn how she went to Jerusalem, and witnessed all the ceremonies of Passion Week,—how she heard short sermons from the bishop and from all the presbyters in turn, proving to us that such exhortations were more common in the Greek Church of the fourth century than they are now,—how she went to the burial-place of Job, and also to Haran, to the very spot where Eleazer met with Rebecca.

The whole diary throws a flood of light on the state of Eastern Christendom before the fall of the Roman Empire, and proves that the love of adventure is by no means a new phenomenon in our sex. This fourth-century narrative of a woman's experience, before a stone of the present venerable monastery was laid, is singularly like our own. Sylvia discovered no manuscripts, for the oldest of those now existing had then hardly begun to be written. She must have carried with her manuscripts of the Pentateuch and of the Books of Kings; and she succeeded in seeing a supposed letter of our Lord to Abgah, King of Edessa.

A more modern coincidence deserves to be noted. For the first two years of our residence in Cambridge we occupied a semi-detached house, and were during that time under the same roof as one of Canon Cureton's married daughters. As my sister could not obtain even a second-hand copy of the Cureton Gospels for love or money, this lady very kindly lent her her father's own copy, to take with us on our second visit to Sinai.

The following lines were written by my sister for her Christmas-card in the winter of 1892:

One more year since Christ was like us
    In a tent of clay;
One year less till He shall take us
    Home for aye.
Oh how bright the path before us!
Oh how great the glory o'er us!
Oh how strong the Hand that tore us
From sin's sway!

One year less of toil and trouble,
    Till we see His face;
Each new step will gain us double
    In our race.
Less and less of tears and sinning,
More and more of work and winning,
Joy that ends in fresh beginning,
    Grace for grace.

CHAPTER V

SECOND VISIT TO SINAI

(From Mrs. Lewis's Journal)

THE STORY of our first visit to Sinai in the pages of the *Churchman* for August had scarcely been finished when an event occurred which made us resolve to return thither within six months. Our readers may remember that we described a Syriac palimpsest, of which the later writing is a martyrology and the earlier one the four Gospels. As my eyes are not keen enough to decipher more than a few separated words of the latter, I took several opportunities of showing the photographs to Syriac scholars, with the result that no one thought they could be read, until I placed a few of the clearest ones in the hands of Mr. F. C. Burkitt. They were shown by him to Professor Bensly, and the two identified the version as of the same type as that discovered by Cureton in 1842, though with considerable variation in the readings. It thus appeared that my efforts had been the means of bringing to light an early text of the Gospels which would supplement the Curetonian one, and be not without value for the light it might throw on disputed passages. A portion of it could be deciphered from my photographs, but the rest was only to be seen from the pages of the manuscript itself. The three gentlemen who undertook to transcribe it, and amongst whom I divided some 360 photographs, Professor Bensly, Mr. Rendel Harris, and Mr. Burkitt, volunteered to go with my sister and me on a joint expedition to Sinai, Mrs. Bensly and Mrs. Burkitt accompanying us.

We spent a few weeks at Cairo, and made three calls on the Archbishop. The first time we went by ourselves, and my sister asked him to allow her to catalogue the Arabic MSS in the convent. She renewed her request when we again called to introduce Professor and Mrs. Bensly, and again when we went with Mr. and Mrs. Burkitt, adding on the third occasion that we should also like to do the Syriac ones. The result was that he wrote a letter to the monks, telling them that the work of cataloguing was to be in our hands only, and that every facility for examining the books was to be given to the party, on condition that we left for the use of the convent copies of the said catalogues in Greek.

Mr. Rendel Harris met us at Suez, and we went into the desert on the 30th January. Dr. Watson had recommended to us a dragoman who was much superior to the one we had last year. Though a Mohammedan, he has always been a *protégé* of the late Dr. Lansing. We were fanned by a cooling breeze, and the road seemed less monotonous than formerly, for it was enlivened by philological discussions, by scraps of song, of wit, and of story. We reached the convent about mid-day on February 8th, were received at the gate by the Bursar, Nicodemus, and conducted to the parlour of Galaktéon the librarian, who now fills the office of Hegoumenos or Abbot.

He received us with a cordiality that was almost overpowering, and was directed chiefly to myself. He hardly knew, in fact, how to express his delight. He kept me behind after the others had left, and told me that he looked on me in the light of his mother, that he would be guided by my advice in everything, and that as four of the party were as yet strangers to him, he would prefer all requests for books, etc., should come to him at first through me.

I, of course, assented to this arrangement, and asked if it would be convenient for us to visit the library in the afternoon.

So we returned at the appointed hour, only too anxious to set our eyes again on the dear old palimpsest. No sooner were we seated than the Abbot entered holding up a blood-stained pocket-handkerchief, and displaying behind it a face and head streaming from recent wounds. His tall cap had fallen off, and his long hair hung down in a helpless fashion. He sank groaning into a chair, and exclaimed, "I have fallen, oh, I am suffering." It was evident that he had been roused to receive us, and when only half awake had gone tilt against the door of the tiny dark closet which does duty for his bedroom. Of course we recommended him to retire to rest, and said we would not trouble him about the library till to-morrow, but he was determined to show it to us, so we were obliged to accompany him thither, he resisting all attempts on the part of the monks and ourselves to put a little plaster on his wounds, which, though many, were only skin deep. But we knew that he had had a serious illness since we were last at Sinai, and notwithstanding his pleasant jest about passing himself off as my son should he ever visit England, he appears to be well over sixty. So we were all not a little anxious lest he should have a feverish night, and delay our friends' chance of beginning work on the palimpsest.

Next morning (Friday) he tottered to what is called the Archbishop's room, where the Syriac books are kept, and asked me what we wished to see first. I replied, "All the books which we photographed last year," and as I had anticipated, the palimpsest and the Jerusalem Lectionary were both produced along with some other Syriac books from a cupboard. I at once asked Galaktéon if he would let me have the Lectionary in my tent, as I wished to work at it myself, and if he would let me have the palimpsest to give employment to my friends. "Just as you wish," was the reply. Whilst I was examining these treasures Mr. Rendel Harris held out another "Jerusalem Lectionary," dated four years later than the one I had discovered, *i.e.* in A.D. 1120, and which is thus the third one of its kind extant. I carried both, with the palimpsest, to our tents, and it may be imagined that the latter at once underwent a critical examination.

Mr. Harris pronounced it to be by no means a difficult palimpsest, but the pages varied greatly in distinctness, and though even I could trace the words (being of their natural size) as I could not do in my photographs, there were many from which the actual ink of the under-writing had faded, leaving only faint indications on the vellum from which words could be traced. Add to this that many of these words were covered by the dark upper-writing which was happily of a different colour and that most of it had to be read between the lines, and my readers may appreciate the difficulty of the task which was to be undertaken. However, after much discussion, the three scholars agreed to the following division of labour. Mr. Rendel Harris to read the first hundred and four pages, Mr. Burkitt the second hundred or more (these included thirty which he had already copied from my photographs) and Professor Bensly the remainder, together with revising as much of the others' work as possible. The Gospels were already known to stop after page 320, as the rest of the palimpsest writing treats of other subjects, partly Syriac and partly Greek. The day was to be divided into three watches, so that some one might be always at work from eight o'clock till eleven, from eleven till two, and from two till five. But as there was a deficiency of bright sunlight after half-past three, and this made a considerable difference to such work, each separate watch was taken in turns on successive days. The manuscript lay in my tent at night, Mrs. Bensly having made a pretty silk cover for it, and was fetched out soon after daybreak in order that Professor Bensly might secure an hour's work before the first watch began. Nor did the coming of darkness bring rest to its pages, for I often sat up till half-past ten to copy some story in the upper-writing after Professor Bensly had finished with it.

We began our work on the catalogues at once. The monks read their Archbishop's letter, and then said that they would never have placed all their treasures in the hands of anyone whom they did not thoroughly know and trust, but that they would most willingly comply with my wish that Mr. Rendel Harris should help me with the Syriac manuscripts, and that one of themselves should relieve my sister from the laborious task of counting the pages of the Arabic ones.

So ten or fifteen volumes were carried up at a time from the various little closets, which are called libraries only by courtesy, and from old chests stored away in the queerest of corners. They lay on the table so that Professor Bensly and Mr. Burkitt might have the opportunity of examining them as soon as we did, and we spent several hours and days in the often very monotonous task of the necessary counting and describing. I left the copying of titles to Mr. Harris, unless a volume looked as if it might prove very interesting, when we searched its pages together.

Mrs. Bensly kindly undertook to count pages for my sister, but the Arabic books so greatly outnumbered the Syriac that the monks also came to her aid, and the little draughty room, with its glassless windows, was sometimes filled with some half-dozen of the holy fathers, counting assiduously under their abbot's directions. They were always greatly pleased when the contents of a book were explained to them. Mr. Harris's thorough knowledge of Church history and of patristic literature proved invaluable in helping us to identify the often strangely sounding and strangely spelt titles of Arabic books.

I had still another project in regard to the palimpsest, which my friends were one and all reluctant to let me disclose, as they did not know how the monks would take it. I had made enquiries in the manuscript room of the British Museum as to

64

the best means of reviving ancient writing, when faded, without risk of injury either to the script or to the vellum. I had come provided with four bottles of a very ill-scented composition, from the fumes of which I hoped to be protected by a respirator specially designed for the purpose.

For ten days I had to restrain my impatience about using this, but on the eleventh I happened to open a large volume of Mar Isaac's discourses which I had known on our former visit, and which contained many pages so faded as to be quite illegible. I asked Galaktéon to let me restore one of these, with the result, that it came up in a brilliant hue of dark green, and he was so astonished that he asked me to paint up the whole volume, then to try my "scent bottle," as it was called, on other hoary documents. How triumphant I felt when he gave me permission to touch up the palimpsest, though only in places where it could not be read otherwise. Professor Bensly at first disapproved of the proceeding, but as both his fellow-workers gave my brush the warmest of welcomes, he was induced after a few days to ask for it himself, and many a blank margin thus became covered with very distinct writing. How many lines were thus restored to the text we cannot well estimate, but in Mr. Harris's portion it might perhaps be a sixth of the whole. Moreover, in difficult passages I was often able to verify the words which one of my friends had deciphered. It was thus that the final colophon came to light, telling that these were the "separated Gospels." The next column probably contains a date, but it baffled all my efforts to bring up more than a few words, and is evidently written with ink which ought to be treated by another chemical.

Mrs. Bensly, besides giving some help to her husband and to my sister, found a sphere of usefulness in trying to teach some Bedawee women to knit. There were two poor creatures who had never known the use of soap and water, who spent most of their time sitting with a couple of children outside the convent gate, and whose home was under a great rock. Their condition was apparently not much above that of the lower animals, and they had had no opportunity of learning anything from one of their own sex. The stupid creatures refused to learn, but some men and boys took up the work so eagerly that their kind teacher could not supply them all with materials.

The three of us who could speak Greek occasionally got into a religious discussion with the monks, especially Nicodemus, who was very anxious to convince us of the good which ascetics had done in the world. "These manuscripts would not be here for you to copy," he would exclaim, "if pious men had not retired into the desert to write them." We thought it wiser not to make the obvious retort, viz. that the monks of the last few centuries had quite failed to comprehend the value of what their predecessors had done. We Presbyterians had rather the advantage over our companions of the Society of Friends and of the Church of England, when we were asked if we accepted the authority of Synods; but we startled Nicodemus by persistently refusing to acknowledge any mediator except the Lord Jesus Christ in our approach to the Father. In discussions with Greek monks, when one gets to a thorny subject, such as the priesthood, a safe plan is to say something about the Pope; this causes a diversion of their energies to an antagonist worth hitting.

The day before our departure a question of mine induced Galaktéon to take us to the coal-cellar, and show us a dark prison-hole, or *oubliette*, to be entered only by a steep ladder. I had no wish to blacken myself, but Mr. Harris went down amidst a shower of farewells in several languages. He found a succession of secret chambers communicating with each other, and Galaktéon confessed to having been once confined there for twenty-four hours, without food, when he had committed a breach of monastic order.

Our journey homewards was a remarkably pleasant one. Heavy showers fell at night, and cooling winds made our rides over the waste enjoyable. The only exception to this was a gust of sand-laden wind which struck suddenly down on us in the Wady esh-Scheikh, and a storm of sand into which we rode between Wady Ghurundel and Sadur.

On the last night of our desert journey three of us hurried on to A'yun Mousa after dinner, that we might be in time to catch the Marseilles boat. Never shall we forget the silent glory of the moon-lit sands, and the ghost-like shadows of the palm trees which told of our approach to civilisation and rest. We could only regret that we had hitherto made no use of these evening hours for travelling, but it is of course impossible to move a camp after it has once settled to the serious business of dining.

It is too soon to tell what the influence of the newly-found Codex will be upon the Canon of Scripture. The last twelve verses of St. Mark's Gospel are conspicuous by their absence, St. Luke beginning on the same page as St. Mark ends. The greeting of the angels to the shepherds in Luke ii, 14 is "Good will towards men." Lastly, our manuscript is linked to the Curetonian by its colophon, which came up under the reviver, and which tells us that these are "the separated Gospels." The Gospels end on page 320 of the manuscript; the remainder is apocryphal writings, in Syriac and in Greek, which are as yet only partly transcribed.

We can only hope that this discovery of an early text of God's great message to the world may lead to an increased interest in Syriac studies, and to a renewed search in Eastern monasteries for further documents, which will, like the "Apology of Aristides," give us a more intelligent insight into the lives of the first martyrs and confessors.

In the Shadow of Sinai

A Story of Travel and Research
from 1895 to 1897

BY

Agnes Smith Lewis

INTRODUCTION

IT IS NOW five years since my twin sister, Mrs. James Young Gibson, published an account of our first and second visits to Mount Sinai in her little book *How the Codex was Found*, a book designed to meet the exigencies of a situation when various incorrect reports concerning the discovery of the Syriac palimpsest had appeared in the press, and when our only means of setting these right was to tell our story as quickly and plainly as possible. The present volume is designed as a sequel to that tale, a narrative of the journeys and adventures which our successful researches entailed upon us in the years following; and it is published with the hope that it may smooth away some of the difficulties which beset the path of those who visit the deserts and the monasteries of the East.

For the sake of those who have not read Mrs. Gibson's book, I begin with a recapitulation or brief account of the discovery.

The project of visiting Sinai came first into my mind in early girlhood, when my future brother-in-law, Mr. James Young Gibson, travelled by Sinai and Petra to Jerusalem in 1865; and his glowing descriptions of desert scenery were for ever haunting my memory. It was revived after a very successful journey which my sister and I made through Greece in 1883. The hospitality which we had received from Greek monks, and the pleasant intercourse which we had enjoyed with Greek ecclesiastics, emboldened me to think that a visit to the Sinai Convent would be profitable, and that perhaps our knowledge of Arabic might facilitate our intercourse with the Bedawîn who would escort us thither. I made an attempt to carry out this design in 1886, but

I got no further than 'Uyûn Musa, being deterred by apprehensions about the health of a lady friend who was travelling with me.

After my marriage in 1887 to the Rev. Samuel Savage Lewis, of Corpus Christi College, Cambridge, we made several Oriental journeys together; but I had to relinquish all thoughts of Sinai, as my husband was bound to residence in his college during February, the only season of the year when a desert journey is compatible with health.

He was taken from me very suddenly in the spring of 1891, and my sister Mrs. Gibson being a widow also, we resolved that our next year's trip should be to Sinai. That summer saw the publication of the Syriac text of the *Apology of Aristides*, which had been discovered by Dr. J. Rendel Harris in the Sinai Library in 1889.

I became so much interested in the volume that I began to learn the Syriac grammar, which a previous knowledge of Hebrew and Arabic made comparatively easy, and I soon found an enthusiastic teacher in the Rev. R. H. Kennett, of Queens' College. Dr. Rendel Harris was then almost a stranger to me, when a chance meeting with his wife led me to tell her that I was studying the Syria of Aristides, and that we intended to visit Sinai. He at once called and insisted not only on teaching us to photograph with his own camera, but gave his opinion so decidedly that there were treasures in the Convent which he had not thoroughly examined, that we both looked forward to our journey with the brightest expectations. For several weeks I constantly dreamt of the dark closet so vividly described to me by Dr. Harris, in which lay the two mysterious chests full of manuscripts, and to which access was only to be obtained by propitiating the reverend recluses who owned them. So strongly were we impressed with the idea that we were going to discover something, that the night before our departure, when the Master of Corpus (Dr. Perowne) and Mr. Kennett both called to say farewell, they actually speculated on what the discovery was to be; and Mr. Kennett expressed a hope that it might be the *Harmony of the Four Gospels* (or Diatessaron) written by Tatian in the second century.

It is also a curious fact that we tried to persuade each of the three scholars to accompany us, who, twelve months later, actually did so for the purpose of transcribing the Syriac Gospels from the palimpsest. But Professor and Mrs. Bensly were bent on a Nile trip, and Mr. Burkitt on a visit to Rome for the sake of editing Tyconius, whilst Dr. Rendel Harris was projecting a visit to Jerusalem and to Athos in the interests of the Cambridge edition of the Septuagint. Dr. Harris very kindly ordered a half-plate camera for us with all its appurtenances, and also designed a manuscript stand for our use to obviate some of the difficulties which he had experienced; and though only one of our photographs as developed by ourselves had really succeeded, we had the courage (or temerity) to provide ourselves with a thousand film-exposures.

We arrived in Cairo on January 14th and obtained, through Lady Scott Moncrieff and the Rev. Nasr Odeh, an private intro-duction to the Patriarch of Alexandria, then represented by the Metropolitan of Libya, and he in his turn gave us his card for the Archbishop of Mount Sinai, to whom we also carried an official letter written in Greek from the Vice-Chancellor of the University of Cambridge (Dr Peile). From both these prelates we received the kindest of welcomes, which was only a foretaste of that accorded to us when we arrived at the Convent on February 6th, after nine days of desert-travel, by the Dikaios, or Prior, and the Librarian, Father Galaktéon. They were delighted at being able to converse with us in their own tongue, and to read my descriptions of their own birthplaces in the Greek edition of my book *Glimpses of Greek Life and Scenery*, and es-pecially did they welcome us as friends of Dr. Rendel Harris. When I was asked "What do you wish to see?" I replied, "All your oldest Syriac manuscripts, particularly those which Dr. Harris had not time to examine, for I want to take a report of them to him."

A few minutes after this daring speech we were taken through a small room containing twelve boxes of MSS, into the dark closet which I had so often dreamt about, and from one of its two little chests some six or eight manuscripts were carried into the light of day. I first examined No. 16, which contained amongst other treatises the long-lost *Apology of Aristides*. Then I saw the palimpsest. It had a forbidding look, for it was very dirty, and its leaves were nearly all stuck together through their having remained unturned probably since the last Syrian monk had died, centuries ago, in the Convent.

I had never before seen a palimpsest, but my father had so often related to us wonderful stories of how the old monks, when vellum had become scarce and paper was not yet invented, scraped away the pages of their books and wrote something new on the top of it; and how, after the lapse of ages, the old ink was revived by the action of common air, and the old words peeped up again; and how a text of Plato had come to light in this curious way.

I saw at once that this manuscript contained two writings, both in the same ancient Estrangelo character, which I had been studying; that the upper-writing was the biographies of women saints, and bore its own date, which I read 1009 years after Alexander, A.D. 697; and that the under-writing was the Gospels. The latter was written in two columns, one of which always projected on to the margin of the upper-writing, so that many of its words could be easily read, and every such word distinctly belonged to the sacred narrative. I pointed this out to my sister, and, as if to make assurance doubly sure, I showed her also that at the top of almost every page stood the title "Evangelium," or "of Matthew," "of Mark," or "of Luke." I felt sure that this text of the Gospels must be at least 200 years older than the one which superseded (or "sat upon" it), and could not therefore be later than the fifth century. It required all my powers of persuasion to make both my sister and Father Galaktéon understand this, for the former did not wish to spend too many films on what might be only legends of saints, and the latter tried to turn my thoughts to a Palestinian Syriac Lectionary of the twelfth century which he thought was very important, and kept wrapped up in a handkerchief. My reasons for placing high value on the palimpsest were noted down in my journal, under the date of February 11th, and were afterwards embodied in an account of our journey which was printed for the *Presbyterian Churchman* of June, July, and August, before we had asked any of our friends to examine the Gospel text.

We returned home about April 1st with a thousand film photographs, 400 of which were those of the Syriac palimpsest, 200 of a codex of Arabic Gospels, 300 of other whole books, viz. a codex of Arabic Epistles,★ the Fathers of the Desert from No. 16,† the Greek Liturgy of St. Mark,‡ a Syriac Liturgy, and the Testament of the Twelve Patriarchs for our friend the Rev. Dr. Sinker, about 100 of desert scenery, and twelve specimen pages from four sources, viz., the Palestinian Syriac Lectionary, two MSS of the Septuagint for Dr. Swete, a Greek Arabic Psalter, and four Georgian MSS.

The development of these films was unavoidably delayed by a dangerous and exhausting illness (surgical erysipelas) which befell my sister, and it was accomplished by ourselves, with the necessary indexing, in the space of six weeks, between June 1st and July 15th. We took every opportunity of telling our friends, especially the Syriac scholars we met with, about the wonderful

---

★ Since published as "Studia Sinaitica," No. II.
† Previously published by pupils of the late Professor Tullberg of Upsala in 1851 under the title "Libri qui inscribitur Paradisus Patrum partes selectae."
‡ The third specimen of its kind extant, transcribed by Mrs. Gibson and sent to a zealous member of the Henry Bradshaw Society.

palimpsest. All our scholar friends, however, including Professor Bensly,★ were too busy to look at our photographs, and the few shown to Dr. Harris on June 11th, just before his departure for the north, were our first attempts at the work.

The idea that they might contain a Curetonian text was expressed by several people, and it made us the more anxious to induce someone to ascertain if this were the case. We were almost in despair about the matter, when the happy idea occurred to us of inviting Mr. and Mrs. Burkitt to luncheon on July 15th, and of asking the former to examine our productions. I picked out the clearest pages from our whole 400, and spread them before him. I explained by what signs I knew the under-writing to be Syriac Gospels of a date not later than the fifth century. He became at once deeply interested and asked me to entrust him with a few to study at home.† I was only too delighted to do so, and forty hours afterwards we received on Sunday morning the following note from Mrs. Burkitt:

"12, HARVEY ROAD.

"My dear Mrs LEWIS,—Frank is in a state of the highest excitement. He wrote down a portion of the palimpsest last night, and has been in to Dr. Bensly with it, and they have discovered it is a copy of the Cureton Syriac. Do you know, only one copy exists! You can imagine Frank's glee! He has just been in to tell me, and has run back to the Benslys'. I thought you would be interested and write at once.—I am, yours affectionately, A. PERSIS BURKITT."‡

★ It was on June 27th, during the Long Vacation, that I asked Dr. Bensly to examine them.
† Several other friends were present, amongst whom were Miss Mary Kingsley, the Rev. Dr. Harmer, now bishop of Adelaide, and the Rev. C. A. E. Pollock, of Corpus Christi College. The two latter, however, left before the examination had gone very far.
‡ See *How the Codex was Found*. The letter was written in haste, and there was a slight inaccuracy in it which was not made known to us till March, 1893.

Mr. Burkitt met Mrs. Gibson at the church door, and showed her a letter written by Professor Bensly to himself. It contained an urgent request that we should all keep the matter secret, so that no one might forestall our Cambridge friends in the transcription of the text. He expressed his opinion that it could be only adequately copied at Sinai itself, and next morning seven of us met by appointment at his house, each one more eager than the other to undertake the journey. My sister and I felt that after Dr. Rendel Harris' great kindness to us, and the unselfish way in which he had directed us towards this discovery, he ought to have an opportunity of taking part in the transcription. Professor and Mrs Bensly cordially welcomed this proposal. The former had often spoken of Dr. Harris' work with sincere admiration, and had himself told us with not a little eagerness of how he had a few months previously proposed Dr. Harris' name for election as a Fellow of his own College. Dr. Harris, soon after in his paleographical lectures, paid a warm tribute to Mr. Burkitt's ingenuity and learning in the matter of the Gospel of Pseudo-Peter, so it seemed as if we could not easily have found a more suitable triumvirate. I divided my photographs amongst them, giving pages 1–104 to Dr. Harris, pp. 104–200 to Mr. Burkitt, and the remainder to Professor Bensly, but of these latter eighty-four pages only contained the Gospel text. This determined the division of the work which they undertook to do at Sinai.

Prof. Bensly's injunctions about secrecy extended to all the other manuscripts which we had photographed. It was broken with regard to the Arabic ones only at the insistence of the late Dr. Robertson Smith, who insisted on my reading a paper about them at the Orientalist Congress which met in the following September. He expressed his opinion very emphatically that entire secrecy would be a mistake, so we put a guarded announcement about the Syriac Gospels in the *Athenaeum* of August 6th.

Mrs. Gibson and I reached Cairo on January 6th, and lost no

time in finding the dragoman, Ahmed 'Abd' er Rahman, whom Professor and Mrs. Bensly, who arrived on January 11th, agreed with us to engage, after they had interviewed some very unsatisfactory rivals. Mr. and Mrs. Burkitt joined us on January 20th, and we had the pleasure of presenting Professor and Mrs. Bensly and them separately to Archbishop Porphyrios, and of interpreting for them, Mrs. Gibson having at a previous interview obtained His Grace's permission for me and for herself to catalogue all the Semitic MSS in the convent. Dr. Harris announced by telegraph his intended arrival, so that we were enabled to include his name in our contract with Ahmed,* and he joined us at Suez on January 27th. The monks received us in a most cordial manner, and at once entrusted the palimpsest to my care. I kept it in my tent, and the three gentlemen were thus enabled to work at copying it for the space of forty days at their tent doors, and they returned home with about four-fifths of the text in their portfolios. But a heavy cloud followed on the bright sunshine. Professor Bensly, whose learning and critical acumen would have been so valuable in the publication of our book, caught a chill when in Rome, and died on April 23rd, only three days after his arrival in Cambridge, whilst Father Galaktéon, to whose kindness we owed so much, followed him into the other world from Sinai a fortnight later.

The result of our friends' labours was given to the world in 1894 by the Cambridge University Press, and it formed quite an epoch in the history of Biblical criticism. The decipherment had not proceeded far when it became evident that this text was not precisely similar to Cureton's. It was of the same character, but more concise, and apparently more ancient by half a century.

---

* This was signed by Professor Bensly on behalf of us all, to avoid the payment of six fees in place of two, a separate fee being charged for each signature. Each of us paid our own share of the expenses in travelling.

Mr. Burkitt supplied some nineteen additional pages belonging to his own portion and to Professor Bensly's, from the fresh photographs which I placed at his disposal, but many gaps were still left in the text, and after I had made an unsuccessful attempt to induce the monks to convey the manuscript to Cairo, and there to allow one or all of the transcribers to fill these up, Mrs. Gibson and I resolved in the spring of 1895 to return to Sinai, and ascertain if anything further could be done with it.

CHAPTER I

PREPARATIONS

WHEN MY sister and I started on our third journey to Mount Sinai in January, 1895, we were in considerable doubt as to whether we should be successful in obtaining access to the Palimpsest of Syriac Gospels. We knew that it had not been shown to visitors in 1894, and we did not know what negotiations concerning its destiny might have been taking place. And if I had cherished the faintest hope of being able myself to read any more of its text, I certainly should not have published an incomplete translation only a few weeks before we left home.

I had sent out a box in 1893 for the safe-keeping of the manuscript. It was made of Spanish mahogany, lined with cedar, and was ornamented with a variety of crosses and Catherine wheels. It had two lids, the inner one of glass so as to admit of its contents being shown without their being handled, and the outer one of wood surmounted by a silver plate bearing an inscription, in Greek uncials, composed by Mr. Charles Moule, of Corpus Christi College:

> "The four Holy Gospels in Syriac. Agnes, the foreigner, has given this casket for the Sacred Scriptures, not without gratitude, to the famous monks."
>
> AGNES SMITH LEWIS

Amidst the tracery of the carved wood-work are various little holes, designed to allow the free passage of air without dust, through the box.

Cairo was at its liveliest during the few weeks of our stay, doing its best to deserve its title of "the gayest capital in Europe." The "Second Army of Occupation," under Generals Cook and Gaze, was in full force, and doing quite as much to hold it in the interests of civilization as the First Army. We had rather an exciting time, for I succeeded in purchasing the little Palestinian Syriac Lectionary, containing readings from the Pentateuch, Prophets, Acts, and Epistles, which I have recently published as No. VI of *Studia Sinaitica*, and this was followed by a still more remarkable incident.

During our visit to Sinai in 1893, Dr. Rendel Harris became painfully impressed by the fact that several important manuscripts which he had seen in 1889 had disappeared from the Convent Library, and this, taken in conjunction with the blanks which Mrs. Gibson and I were obliged to leave in our Syriac and Arabic Catalogues, led him to suspect and declare openly that several thefts must have taken place since his previous visit. He had photographed a few pages of a beautiful sixth-century manuscript of II, III, IV. Maccabees, and he readily fell in with my suggestion that any of these pages should be appended to my Syriac Catalogue as its frontispiece, in the hope that its whereabouts, and possibly its thief, might be detected. An itinerant dealer in antiquities happened to call on us in the hotel one Sunday afternoon; he placed an Arabic MS in Mrs. Gibson's hands and a Syriac one in mine. The moment I opened it my glance fell on a couple of pages exactly similar to the frontispiece of my newly published book. There was the title at the top of each page "Maccabai," there were the dirty water marks where the book had once been wet, and as I stepped to the table and turned over the first leaf of my book so as to put the two side by side, I could see the most minute yellow stains on the pages of the MS exactly reproduced in my frontispiece. There were only two people in the world who could have recognised this at a glance, Dr. Harris and myself. I cut short my sister's negotiations with the dealer by saying we were going to church, and that he must allow us to keep the manuscripts till Monday so that we might make up our minds about them. We at once took steps to denounce the matter to an agent of the Mixed Tribunals, and with our consent the manuscript was seized in our rooms, a *procès-verbal* being drawn in the name of Archbishop Porphyrios, so that the affair might be decided during our absence in the desert. It was followed by a lawsuit between the monks and the dealer who had bought the manuscript from the thief, and was decided in favour of the latter, owing chiefly to a mistake in the *procès-verbal* made by the monks' solicitor, who had not understood the English of my Preface to the Catalogue, and had imagined that the frontispiece was from a photograph taken by me instead of by Dr. Rendel Harris in 1889. As the MS bore such a strong resemblance to the facsimile, the Mixed Tribunal must have had a difficulty in deciding as they did. Perhaps they were influenced by the consideration that the purchaser of stolen property, having parted with his money to the thief, is entitled to some compensation if dispossessed by the owner.

This incident gave rise to a paragraph in the *Egyptian Gazette*, which was copied into some French papers, to the effect that the Palimpsest of the Syriac Gospels had been recognised by Mrs. Gibson and me in the hands of a Cairo dealer. It was all the while safe at the Convent.

We could not come to terms with Ahmed, who had made us on the whole very comfortable in 1893, because he wanted quite fifty pounds more than we had paid to Hanna in 1892. Mr. Aulich, the manager of the Hotel d'Angleterre, found another dragoman for us at once, a young Druse named Joseph Scha'ar, a Protestant by religion, who had spent a year in the American College at Râs Beyrout, and was a grade above both Hanna and

Ahmed in point of education. He had never before visited Sinai, but in our case that was of little consequence, and he adapted himself to Bedawy notions as if to the manner born.

And here I must make a few notes as to ways and means. The charge for each camel, going to and returning from the Convent, is five pounds. Baedeker says that it may be done for less, but as the tariff is fixed by agreement between the Bedawîn and the monks, this is impossible. As all our provisions for fifty days had to be carried, we required eleven camels for the two of us on our first journey, four for riding, and the rest for baggage, the dragoman and the cook being of course mounted.* The sheikh's camel made a twelfth, but for that Hanna did not pay. The sheikh, or head man, is appointed for each trip by the camel-drivers themselves out of their own number. He is in no sense the sheikh of a tribe, for each man has a right to the office when his turn comes, and this is regulated according to the tribes which compose your escort. In 1892 and 1893 each of the four tribes which inhabit the Peninsula took it in turns to supply travelling parties with camels, and therefore our escort was quite homogeneous, sitting round the same camp-fire at night. Payments to the Bedawîn are supposed to be made through the sheikh, but sometimes they do not trust him, and will ask the dragoman to distribute the money himself. A peculiarity in this case is that the Bedawîn insist on all payments being made beforehand. Unless they have received your money they will not work. They do so to protect themselves, for there is one case authenticated of a dragoman who had escorted a party to Dinai and back, taking the train at Suez and the steamer to France without having paid a penny to the camel owners. These had no redress, for they do not acknowledge the jurisdiction of the Egyptian courts, and the only powers to whom they ever appeal to settle their disputes are the Prior or the Economos of the

* In 1893 we had thirty camels for seven travellers.

Convent, who in this instance could not help them. The Convent levies a tax of ten francs on every camel engaged, and this it pays over to two old sheiks in Cairo, who watch over the interests of their fellow tribesmen. In what way it is applied I have been unable to discover. Dragomans, when negotiating with you about expenses, make a great point of the fees which they have to pay to the Convent for the "ground-rent" of encamping in the garden, and for other privileges. I believe that £7 covered the whole of the fees which were paid on our behalf in 1897.

My sister and I had only two tents when we travelled alone, one of which did duty as bed-room and dining-room, and a kitchen-tent, in which the dragoman and the cook both slept. The former waited on us, as in duty bound, at meals. He was by far the most important member of our caravan, for on his energy, tact, and judgement the success of the expedition, in a material sense, depended. Our first dragoman, Hanna, was a swarthy native of Syria, with a black curled moustache, and an amusing little swagger, which suited well with the suit of bright blue cloth which he wore. He was a Roman Catholic, and his chief defect was that he gave us, quite unwittingly, a wrong account of the religion of the Bedawîn, an account opposed to the view of all who have studied them closely. They have no form of worship, he averred, even at the burial of their dead, and they had no ideas of time beyond the two words *el yaum* ("to-day") and *bukra* ("to-morrow"). Hanna quite believed his own statement, and this should be a caution to all Eastern travellers, that they must take into account the religion of their informant before they place implicit faith in his reports of the religion of the other people.

It was very curious, however, that Hanna and Joseph Scha'ar, who are Christians, knew much better how to manage the Bedawîn than Ahmed, who is a Moslem. Ahmed is very clever and trustworthy, but he had visited Sinai only once before, in his boyhood, as servant to the late Rev. Dr. Lansing, and he began to order the camel drivers with the overbearing manner which a Mohammedan Egyptian is accustomed to use to Christians and to inferiors. The Bedawîn would not stand this, and when in 1893 we encamped on the second night in Wady Sadur they refused to help in pitching our tents, with the result that nothing was ready when we arrived; neither coffee nor hot water for washing, nor the rudiments of dinner, and we had to wait for half-an-hour in Mr. Burkitt's tent before our own was set up, everything being in a confusion such as we had never before experienced in any of our journeys. On more than one evening, Ahmed brought his money-bags to us for safe keeping, telling us that a woman's tent was the only place where they were perfectly secure.

This made us feel uncomfortable, for it put upon us the responsibility which we were actually paying him to relieve us of; and we did not comprehend the matter till some time afterwards. After we left 'Ain Howarah, he recognised his mistake and had the sense to make a complete change in his manner of addressing the Bedawîn. He seemed to us in fact, rather too deferential, for he never gave an order without the formula *'amilni el-m'arûf* ("do me the favour"). I know another excellent dragoman who, when he loses control of his temper, bestows a savage kick on his own canteen. I do not quite see the utility of this proceeding, but it has one advantage, for the canteen harbours no grudge against him.

However much experience an Arab dragoman may have in travelling with tents, it is a safe rule never to allow him to take out your railway ticket, not to let him register your luggage. Living, as he probably does in the Lebanon, or on the banks of the Nile, he can have no experience of these matters, and it is safer to entrust them to the hotel *portier*. I speak feelingly, for we once nearly lost our camera and all our other hand luggage at the Cairo station, and again our train wholly at the Suez one, through the original ideas of dragomans. In one case it was supposed that our effects must be stowed away in carriages other than the one we travelled by, lest they should incommode us; and in the other, the name of our destination was indeed given, but it was not that of a station on the railway, it was not even in Africa.

All dragomans have much to learn about the way to seat a woman comfortably on a camel, and indeed the knowledge only came to ourselves after many trying experiences. I will not inflict these on my readers, but will content myself with stating a few elementary facts.

The saddle on which you have to sit is not far removed from a common baggage one, and in many cases actually is one. It has two horns, one of which is meant for a rough support to your back, but if it be too short, it will rather act as a prod. Your knees ought to rest on either side of the front horn, and you ought to be able to cross your feet in front of it, but sometimes from the angle at which you are sitting you find this an impossibility. The animal's back is protected from the rubbing of the saddle by a pad filled with rough straw, whose points are as sharp as nails if they come in contact with your ankles. On the saddle itself a gay looking quilted cover is generally placed; its looks are the best of it, for the stuffing is of the thinnest cotton, and quite half the fatigue and discomfort of camel-riding is due to this. Also, to keep you steady, your toe is thrust into a rope stirrup, and whether it be long or short, your whole leg gets cramped, for you are unable to change its position or that of its fellow at will.

It was a great day when we discovered how to remedy all this. The rule is simple. *Observe what your dragoman has got for himself, and adopt it.* After all, the structure of his bodily frame does not differ greatly from your own, and why should he have four folds of a thick bed-quilt, and a pillow to boot, beneath him, while you have only one fold of a thing whose stuffing is of the scantiest? The pillow has the advantage of filling up the round hole in the centre of your saddle. We have discovered that all arrangements like arm chairs are a mistake, for they restrict your power of turning around, and that stirrups are still greater blunders. A man is infinitely better off than a woman, for unless he be of heavy build he can vary his position by sitting side-ways or with his face to the camel's tail. There is also the position of horns to be considered. These are sometimes placed so close to each other that they afford too scanty room for the rider's person, and when this is done to a traveller who is no longer young, and who has mounted a camel for the first time, my only wonder is that he or she does not give up the journey at once.

These things need not be. Oriental apathy ought to give way before the elementary wants of travellers who bring money and employment to the natives of so desolate a region; and either the dragomans, or Messrs. Cook and Gaze, ought to design a camel saddle which will not be so hap-hazard in its structure.

The Archbishop was then at Sinai, but in Cairo we exchanged visits with his representative, a young priest who had studied for two years at Leipzig with some distinction, as we were afterwards assured by one of his German fellow-students whom we met in Jerusalem. We had also a long conversation with the Holy Deacon Nicodemus, formerly Economos of the Convent, who had been stationed for the last two years at Suez. He is a man of some administrative capacity, and has written some clever articles for Athenian papers in confutation of all mountain tops, save Jebel Musa, and their claim to be the Mount of the Law, and on the paramount authority of tradition as opposed to modern criticism. But he was not equal to Galaktéon in his knowledge of the Greek manuscripts in the Convent. Dr. Rendel Harris gave him great credit in 1893 for the neat way in which the fences and everything pertaining to the Convent garden were kept. Nicodemus spoke French well, and where he really shone was when travellers and dragomans were making their arrangements with a fresh set of Bedawîn to conduct them from Sinai to Jerusalem. He would stand for hours arguing with a set of excited, ruffianly looking men, displaying the utmost coolness and patience.

Nicodemus seemed greatly to enjoy the idea of what was in store for us at the convent, and to be suppressing an account of something to which he alluded more by glances than by words.

We took the train to Suez on January 28th, and alighted at our old quarters in the Greek Hotel d'Orient. The landlord, Mr. Philippides, is an elderly man, a native of Cephalonia, whose youth passed away before the establishment of elementary schools in Greece, and who is therefore ignorant of both reading and writing, though he speaks his own language and Italian with correctness and fluency. The head waiter is usually un-lettered also, but they have always been particular in requesting Mrs. Gibson to write out in Greek a detailed receipt for all luggage confided to their charge during our absences at Sinai. The house is more distinguished for its cleanliness than its cookery, and the Greek boy-servants are both extremely good-natured and obliging. Of all this I was destined to have further experience.

Some half-dozen of the monks who happened to be staying at Suez called on us, and Father Daniel, a young man who has some command of French, and had been librarian for a short time after Galaktéon's death, was only prevented from accompanying us because he could not get a camel in time. He was therefore obliged to go with his companions in a sailing boat to Tor.

We tried to take that route ourselves, by ordering one of the Khediviale Company's boats, which ply to the Red Sea ports as far as Suakim, to stop at Tor for us. But they asked for £25 besides the usual passage money for ourselves and servants; moreover the agent was so long in answering our letter that we had made our contact with the Bedawîn before we heard of his proposal.

The Archbishop and the monks had made a new arrangement

with the Bedawîn for the conveyance of travellers, and it had come into force for the first time when the Archbishop went to the Convent in 1894. In place of the four tribes, Jebaliyeh, Sowalha, Beni Saeed, and Alizat, each taking charge of a party for the whole journey, and having the right to do so by turns, each party is now conveyed by a mixed company composed of all four tribes. Only the Sowalha were absent personally from our number, being all occupied in their lucrative possession, the turquoise mines; but some of their camels were there, led by a man of the Beni Saeed. Each tribe in turn has a right to appoint the sheikh or head camel driver for a party, who remains sheikh till the end of that trip. Five pounds continues to be the hire of a camel from Suez to Sinai and back, but if nine days be exceeded on the up journey, or seven on the down one, each day has to be paid for extra. A Sunday's complete rest, or a day at Feirân, is not charged for by the Bedawîn, but if their camels be employed at all on these rest days they are considered to be full working days. I strongly objected to seven days only being allowed for the return. It is far too little for most women, and indeed for many men who have not passed their childhood on camels, and if the Bedawîn wish to attract travellers they will make haste to rescind this rule. We simply ignored it, and contracted with Joseph for ten days, including a Sunday, on the return journey.

CHAPTER II

ON THE TRACK OF THE ISRAELITES

WE CROSSED the Red Sea from Port Tewfik to the deserted quarantine station on the afternoon of January 31st in a small sailing boat, accompanied by shoals of great fish which often leapt out of the water. The Arabs called them Abu Salaam, and said that they boded luck, but we could not tell whether they were sharks or dolphins. Half-an-hour's walk brought us to 'Uyûn Musa. The night was cold and windy, but Joseph's tents were remarkably comfortable.

'Uyûn Musa consisted at that time of only two gardens, planted chiefly with palm trees around a few brackish wells, and some plots sewn with vegetables. These were the property of Mr. George Athanasios, owner of the Red Sea Stores at Suez, and agent there for the Sinai Convent. A somewhat roughly built house serves for the accommodation of his family during the heat of summer. Most of the year it has no sign of life about it, for the kitchen stove is unlighted, and the three little bedsteads in an inner room are rarely offered to a benighted traveller. A cool verandah before the front door is furnished with tables and benches. We were invited to rest on some divans, or rather settles, inside of this, and here the *wakeel*, or steward, placed cushions around us and treated us to some delicious coffee. He, with three fellaheen gardeners and two half nomadic Bedawy families, are the sole inhabitants of the oasis. The little cemetery on the sandy bank outside contains only a dozen graves. Nothing, indeed, can be bought in the place, except, possibly, a little coffee from the Bedawîn outside.

It would be difficult to imagine a more lonely spot. The beauty of the dark waving foliage is greatly enhanced by the utter dreariness of the sandy waste which surrounds it. The only human habitation near is quite two miles away. The quarantine station on the shore of the Red Sea, which has lately been greatly enlarged, at the period of our first three visits did not shelter even a care-taker. On three sides stretches an undulating plain of soft yellow sand, which must be traversed for days before you can see another human dwelling, for it is absolutely without water.

When the quarantine station is occupied, its inmates are not allowed to approach the oasis, so that travellers may there pitch their tents freely, without fear of infection. The same remark may be made about Tor and the station in its vicinity, where the pilgrims returning from Mecca receive a much needed cleansing.

'Uyûn Musa, the Wells of Moses, is supposed to be the spot where Miriam raised her song of triumph, "Sing unto the Lord, for he hath triumphed gloriously; the horse and his rider hath He cast into the sea." If the Israelites crossed the Red Sea near Suez, or even if they crossed it much higher up on the line of the present canal, 'Uyûn Musa would be their first natural stopping place, for there only could they get a drop of drinking water. How delighted we were to step into our tent after the long weary waiting, and to sit on the soft carpet and eat the well-cooked dinner which Joseph's care had provided for us. There was something charming even in the thought of dwelling for nearly two months on the clean sand, so much pleasanter than the floor and other appurtenances of many a so-called "Grand Hotel" in the islands or mainland of Greece. We had contracted for three courses at dinner—soup, meat and pudding. We think this is quite sufficient where everything has to be carried, though most travellers in Palestine have two kinds of meat; but in the desert what can the dragoman give you for a variety, unless it be salted and tinned things, provocative of thirst, if not of indigestion? We had as many oranges and dates as we wanted. Eggs were carried packed in common salt, and they remained fresh to the very last, though when we tried the same process at Cambridge they all went bad. The desert air keeps everything sweeter than it would be elsewhere. Plenty of tinned vegetables and farinaceous foods may be bought in the Cairo shops and at the Red Sea Stores in Suez. The former are almost a necessity in the dry air of the desert. Ahmed quite forgot our injunctions to provide them in 1893. He tried, indeed, to feed us on an almost exclusively flesh diet, varied by plum puddings, for the first ten days of our journey, a regimen which was sorely trying to the dyspeptic amongst us, and was especially hard on our one vegetarian. This is a mistake into which I have frequently seen Oriental hotel-keepers fall. Vegetables are cheap in Cairo and in Jerusalem. They are therefore not good enough for European gentry, and you grind the most stringy of meat, trying to like it, whilst a few doors off magnificent cauliflower and asparagus lie in the shops as if under a ban. Ahmed, in consequence of our complaints, had to buy vegetables from the Convent garden, but he must have paid a high price for them.

Poultry is carried in crates on the backs of camels. It has the additional advantage of providing you with fresh eggs when you give the hens a long enough rest. Mutton and gazelle may frequently be procured at Sinai, especially when there has been some rain in the winter, a sheep costing from 20 to 25 francs.

We were awakened next morning by what Mrs. Gibson called "our patent Egyptian alarm clock," the crow of a little cock. We never allowed the Bedawîn to take down our tent till we had quite finished breakfast, and had both issued from it fully equipped for our ride. This is a point of some importance for the comfort of lady-travellers, and report has told us that is is not always regarded in the great Palestine caravans. The first morning's start is generally made amidst a scene of the wildest confusion and quarrelling, everyone shouting and gesticulating in a frantic way over the load that has been assigned to him, the dragoman scolding them all by turns, and the camels roaring like mad things, whilst the sheikh goes about and tries to bring them all to reason. When peace seems secure they will again fall to disputing afresh over some small package which no one will accept, and which varies in value from a tin basin to a camera. This is an inveterate habit of theirs, and it has usually to be settled by the dragoman taking the package on his own camel. In 1894 they had acted in a precisely similar manner with a valise belonging to their suzerain lord, the Archbishop, and a monk had to carry it on his shoulder for two days, till they grew ashamed of themselves.

My sister and I did not wait for this ceremony, but started at 7.30, and walked over the sand till 8.45, when Joseph and the camels came up. This was much quicker work than we had before experienced. We reached the edge of the great plain at 10.30, whereas with Hanna we had taken five hours to cover the same distance.

Joseph explained to us his method. He had neither bullied the Bedawîn, nor stormed at them, nor argued with them, but, in imitation of the Rev. Dr. Bliss' manner with his students, he had taken out a pencil and a note-book, and begun to write down all that was being said and done. This was too much for our suspicious friends; they have some vague idea of a Recording Angel, and they did not know what mysterious power these notes would have over them in the future. So they tied on their burdens in peace.

A camel becomes an intensely interesting being when he is carrying you. You observe that the yellow hue of his skin is exactly that of the sand, whilst the dark brown of his shaggy mane and the hairy fringe of his tail match well with the rocks in the wadys. You regard the elastic spring of his spongy foot, the not ungraceful twists of his long massive neck, with as much interest as you are wont to bestow on the telegraphic column of your newspaper at home, and all his humours become as important for the moment as the last piece of gossip in your visiting circle. My friend Dr. Macalister, the Professor of Anatomy at Cambridge, assures us that the notion of this ungainly creature having an extra joint in his legs or a series of water-tanks in his stomach is long-ago exploded. He has dissected the creature and has found no such thing. What gives rise to the idea of an extra joint is simply that he can bend his leg at the shoulder-blade in either way, whereas a horse can do so only in one. And he perspires so little that he is not in constant need of the water which he so greatly enjoys when he gets it. His supreme virtue is his patience, and his ability to subsist on the dry desert herbage at which even a thistle-loving donkey would turn up its nose. There was one little plant which we saw frequently as we were passing through the hilly region. It grew straight out of the sand, like its neighbours, without any mould about it, and it had not a single leaf, but only a green stem and little branches furnished with spikes as strong and sharp as two-inch iron nails. My camel would actually turn from the bunch of tempting herbs which Aâgi, his master, was holding before his nose as he walked, to crunch up this dreadful thing, and he would pick it out of preference to anything else when he was unheeded. I have even seen him devour actual wood, the leafless bough of a palm tree, and look as if he considered it a treat.

Camels are, as is well known, not responsive to kindness. You cannot caress them, for the least touch on their heads or necks when you are dismounted, will bring their teeth into your arm. The reason for this is that their masters are in the habit of punishing them by beating them on the neck. I have only once seen this done, and it was not by one of our own people. The thunder of growls which accompanied it was terrific.

Mounting and dismounting is much more troublesome than riding. We never accomplished this feat without the precaution of having either the dragoman or a Bedawy to stand beside us. Yet it is not really difficult. The important thing is to lean backwards, for you are in more danger of getting pitched over the camel's head than over his tail. And I had got so accustomed to the business, that in this our third trip to Sinai I sometimes hardly noticed that my camel was kneeling till I found myself near the ground.

The camel's great dislike to kneeling is a special comfort to novices. His master has to tug at the rope round his nose and actually bring his head to the ground before the obstinate creature will bend his legs, and the hoarse gurgling noise which runs through the long neck testifies that he does so under compulsion. You may therefore stand, or rather sit, on your camel quite at your ease while your friend stops to have his or her saddle adjusted, for you will not be projected off by any sudden freak on the part of your mount. If your first ride has been of any length, you will have an almost intolerable pain in the small of your back for several days and nights, but this will gradually wear away, and you will find it greatly relieved by walking, though the only effectual cure for it is sleep. It is of course caused by muscles coming into play which have never before been used, and it therefore will not recur for some time at least. In my subsequent visits to the desert, with a year's interval between each, I cannot recollect that I suffered from it at all.

It was evident that we were going to have more fun with the Bedawîn than we had enjoyed on our former journeys. Notwithstanding their poor primitive clothing, one and all have bright good-natured faces with flashing black eyes, and many of them walk with the dignity of patriarchs. Most of these men have only one means of livelihood—their camels. Each possesses one, and on its hire he depends for his daily bread and that of his family. If he should acquire a second camel, he is considered rich, but he is never likely to have three, for if his wife should notice that he is making money she will do her utmost to thwart him. She well knows that if he should earn enough, he will take a second wife, younger and prettier than herself, and her hope of domestic happiness will be gone. I have heard the same story in Algeria, and there it was assigned as the reason why Christian families are generally more prosperous than Moslem ones.

The difficulty which we had experienced with the Bedawy dialect was not a mere difference of words, though that certainly exists, but a very serious one of pronunciation. I have not yet got at all its peculiarities, though my ear is now more accustomed to its sound. For instance, if a Bedawy wants his camel to rise, instead of saying "*Cum*" (get up), he says "*Geem*," (the *g* being hard as in *give*). And he calls the moon *"Gamar"*. If in 1892 we did not understand all the Bedawîn said, we were greatly entertained by Hanna's talk to them. It consisted of disquisitions on his own cleverness, and the general inferiority of themselves to the rest of the world, but it had a strong flavour of human sympathy in it, and frequently of wit.

It was from his lips, whilst addressing the cook, that we caught a phrase which I have named the ordinary dragoman's creed: "*Ana a'raf, wa anta la ta'raf*" (I know every[thing], and thou knowest no[thing]). And it was very pleasant to hear him discuss with the Bedawîn the improvement which the British occupation of Egypt has wrought in the condition of the fellaheen, and the contrast between the rule of our people and that of the French in Algeria.

A great source of interest to us arose from the presence amongst them of Mrs. Gibson's camel-driver, a man of much force of character, named Mushaghghil.* He was conspicuous

---

* This may be translated "He who keeps others always busy", or "always on the go," and it is an accurate description of his character.

amongst his brethren by his ruddy face and by the flash of his
black eyes, which harmonised well with the faded red blanket
which he wore over his shoulders instead of a goat hair *abbaya*,
and which was replaced by a brilliant new one on Sundays. He
loved to make Mrs. Gibson pronounce his name at all times,
especially when she was alighting from her camel, and watched
eagerly whether or no she would stumble over the formidable
double guttural in the middle of it. I am tempted to give some
of the rules for Arabic pronunciation which I have heard from
educated natives, in the hope that some of my readers may profit
by them.

In addition to the "cheth", which we have in the Scottish
"loch," and to the plain ordinary English *h*, this ancient and
lovely tongue possesses four gutturals to which the vocal organs
of Europeans have never been accustomed.

I. The *ghain,* or *gh*, a combination of *g* and *r*, is formed by an
elevation of the soft palate from whose roof it issues. It is said to
be the first sound uttered by a baby camel, along whose long
tender throat it must roll magnificently. To achieve it you are
directed to imagine yourself about to gargle, or be sea-sick. I
once happened to remark to a native that the *ghain* was like the
voice of the camel, and he at once replied, "Like the voice of
the nightingale."

II. The *'ain*, represented by a rough breathing, is also formed
in the soft palate. I have found it more difficult to acquire than
any other Arabic consonant, and I lose it when I am not in the
country. As the same letter exists in Hebrew, I once asked a
learned Rabbi how he pronounced it. He replied, "I fetch a long
breath and I turn up my nose, and then it comes easily." The
Arabs have no difficulty with it, but Europeans are tempted to
slur it over.

III. The dotted *q̈* which we have in Qurân, and which we may
represent by the letter *C*. This is produced with a jerk in the soft
palate, and the Egyptians give the jerk without the actual letter.

IV. The soft *h*, for which we have no equivalent in Europe. It enters into the structure of numberless words, and if you pronounce it like an ordinary *h* the Arabs won't understand you. When once acquired it is not easily forgotten. It is sounded what I call "on the breath" as it issues from the mouth, but it is nevertheless said to come from a deeper part of the chest than any of the others. It is equivalent to the Hebrew *He*, a particularly sacred sound, because they say that by it God made the worlds.

The path which we traversed in the afternoon ran along a stony plain, from which we could see to our left the chain of low barren hills which bound the region of the Tîh (Wandering), and to our right the mountains of Africa beyond the bright blue waters of the Red Sea. One cannot keep up a conversation on camel-back without some exertion of the voice, and reading is out of the question; so we had plenty of time to meditate. As my brother-in-law, James Young Gibson, remarked, this has been the scene of one of the most stupendous miracles recorded in Scripture, and the one for which there is the clearest historical evidence. You cannot account for the history and traditions of the Jews without acknowledging that Moses did lead them out of Egypt into Palestine. To deny this would be almost to upset the very basis on which history rests. And if Moses did so, how could the people possibly be fed without supernatural intervention? To take twenty people to Sinai with all the modern appliances of tinned meat, Swiss milk, etc., is a feat; to provide for the wants of two, taxes the ingenuity of a clever dragoman, and here were several thousands with women, children, babies, and flocks. The flocks no doubt waxed smaller through being eaten into, and there probably was more vegetation than now in the mountain districts and at oases, such as Elim. But after making all allowances, we still have to take into account the two-and-a-half or three days of perfectly waterless sand between 'Uyûn Musa and Wady Ghurundel.

98

We spent our Sunday at Wady Ghurundel (Elim), a broad shallow valley several miles long, filled with sandy mounds, torf bushes, and palms, which have sprouted again from the stumps of their cut and burnt predecessors. A bivouac of Bedawîn will often in a single night destroy that which was a joy to the eye and a shadow from the heat to every passing traveller. There are several bubbling springs, whose water, though palatable to the camels, is quite unfit for human beings, as it contains, amongst other delicacies, a strong infusion of Epsom salts. Near Ghurundel is a lofty hill called Hammam Far'aôn, the hot bath of Pharaoh, whose unquiet spirit, the Arabs believe, sends up from the bed of the Red Sea the boiling sulphur springs near its summit. These springs have proved efficacious for the cure of rheumatism.

A Sunday in the desert is a glorious thing. You can enjoy the luxury of lying a little longer in bed, with no stern sense of duty compelling you to rise. The rest is doubly sweet after the fatigue you have undergone, and you have leisure to appreciate fully the romantic character of your surroundings. You watch the camels browsing lazily on the thorny plants, and their swarthy masters roasting coffee in the smouldering embers of a brush-wood fire; you amuse yourself with the clever little hens picking up crumbs within the sacred precincts of the kitchen tent, as if they had a burning desire to step into the stew-pan; you look from them over the vast expanse of sand, or up to the high frowning cliffs on whose brow desolation has set its seal; and you drink a deep draught of quiet with the pure crisp air you are breathing, far away from telegraph, post-office, newspapers, and the myriad distractions of civilized life. The ground on which you are camping has witnessed the passage of the Israelites which you have been reading about in your Bible, and the unseen presence of the Deity who revealed Himself to them is still about you.

Our difficulties about water had now come to an end. Mrs.

Gibson, mindful of her sufferings in this part of our first journey, conceived the ingenious plan in 1893 of taking twelve bottles of St. Galmier water, the first half of which she shared with the whole party between Suez and Wady Ghurundel, and the second half she wished to bury at Ghurundel itself (with perhaps a written curse on the unwarranted disturber of it), and to dig it up for use on our return journey between Ghurundel and Suez. It was difficult to hammer the idea into Ahmed's head. He declared at Ghurundel that the remaining six bottles had got mixed with our friends' wine bottles, and that he could not get access to them without the Bedawîn knowing it. When we reached Ethâl, I insisted on his separating them and carrying them on our own riding camels till we should find a convenient spot in which to deposit them; and Mr. Burkitt very kindly gave his services in digging, two tent-pegs being stuck into the ground above them. Five of us promised to recollect the spot when we should return, from the shape of the hills that faced it, with the result that no two of us could agree in identifying it when the time for digging up the bottles arrived, and my sister was entitled to boast that her memory had been better than mine.

In 1895 and 1897 we buried three bottles only at Ghurundel itself, and found them untouched on our return journey from Sinai. A travelling filter is indispensable till you reach the Wady Mukattab. We spent Sunday there in 1893, and the Bedawîn, to avoid the labour of carrying water from a place half-a-mile away, disclosed to Ahmed one of their tribal secrets—the existence of one of the finest springs of water in the peninsula, quite near to our camp.

I have tried the little soldier's filter, and it is excellent for one person only, as the water is sucked through it. Maignen's cottage filters for household use are delightful, for you can change the charge of charcoal yourself; but a travelling one I bought from him spilt all its black contents over my clothes in a new trunk.

A Berkefeld filter proved to be a success in Mr. Burkitt's hands, but it has never done so in mine. I now give the palm to Pasteur's, which is portable, efficient, and easily managed by a lady, seeing that it requires care rather than strength.

Our Bedawîn had a furious quarrel on Monday before we started. Mushaghghil appeared to be the leader of it, for as he stood gesticulating amongst the other men, his eyes seemed as if they would start out of his head with passion. From a genial merry fellow he seemed transformed into a wild demon. They all threw their swords and guns down in a heap on the sand, as a signal that they must appeal to an umpire. Joseph then stepped in and said that they could settle the quarrel in the evening after our journey's end, for they were losing the best part of the day. They took his advice, and picked up their weapons. When evening came they were slow to re-commence; for they were tired, and their passions had cooled.

Our sheikh Sariya was of the Alizat tribe and so is Mushaghghil. My camel-driver was of the Beni Saeed, and so was Joseph's, though he rode a camel of the Sowalha. We had thus three camp fires round our tents, for they all ate separately. The Jebaliyeh or "serfs of the court," to whom our ex-sheikh and quondam scullion, Mohammed, belonged, are not considered true Arabs, but descendants of Hungarian immigrants whom the Empress Helena brought to the peninsula. The other tribes will not inter-marry with them. Mushaghghil is not related to the ruling family of his tribe, and has no chance of ever being its sheikh; nevertheless he has a determining voice in its government, as indeed he had in that of our little caravan, for Sariya was next to nowhere beside him.

One afternoon during our return journey I was riding a little ahead, when I heard a lively discussion going on behind me, interrupted by merry shouts. I overheard "twenty guineas" being repeated several times, and "too much, too much." I was puzzled to know what it could be about, for Mushaghghil's face was beaming with happiness, his shapely stalwart form seemed more erect, and his step more elastic than usual. The men could not therefore be discussing some imposition of the tax-gatherer, and Joseph's look of indifference showed that it was not a matter that concerned him.

He was riding almost alongside of me, and I asked him what the Bedawîn were talking about. "Mushaghghil is engaged to be married," replied Joseph, "and he is inviting all our men to the wedding feast. He will have to spend about twenty pounds in buying his bride from her father, providing her with clothes, and killing sheep for the banquet." "But where will he get the twenty pounds?" I asked, for Mushaghghil's scanty clothing and habits of life gave no indication of such wealth.

"Oh, he has money laid by. But don't imagine that it's his first marriage. He has a wife already about his own age, but they quarrelled and she returned to her father's house. Mushaghghil said, 'I won't divorce her, because that would be giving her what she wants, leave to marry again, but I'll take her if she comes back.' Then their friends interfered and made peace. There was a reconciliation, and she came back. But they quarrelled again, and she went to her father's house the second time. Then Mushaghghil said: 'How am I to get her back? I can't demean myself by going and begging her to come. I won't live alone, so I shall just marry again; and if she returns, her punishment is to be that she will be the servant in the house where she was mistress.'"

I could not help wondering how many of our English grooms at home, or our workmen, could afford to expend twenty pounds on the occasion of their weddings, and to do it likewise for the second time in their lives. I asked the age of the bride-elect.

"Fifteen," was the reply.

Mrs. Gibson expressed her conviction that not one of the three who were to comprise Mushaghghil's future household would be happy. "If he disagrees with his young wife about anything," she said, "he will seek sympathy from the older one, and both will be afraid to contradict him. They will be jealous of each other, and true love will be a stranger to their tent."

We did not feel free to congratulate the happy bridegroom, but we told him that he was about to do what would be impossible in our country. The Bedawîn were of course not ignorant on this subject, but they seemed to have a difficulty in grasping the idea that a man could be content with one wife unless forced to it by poverty. "If I could afford it," said Mushaghghil, "I would marry again every year." His companions heard this with a delighted acquiescence.

Mohammedans often tell Europeans that they have only one wife, because they perceive that this enhances their reputation, but they do not lift the curtain from their past. Our old dragoman, Ahmed, for instance, has now a pretty young wife, to whom he is devotedly attached, but her two childless predecessors, whom he has divorced, are still alive.

I did not take so kindly to camel riding as I had done in 1893. I was very often tired, and had to lie down the whole of the time that we rested after lunch. The Bedawîn were greatly concerned about this. In the Wady Mukattab they determined to find out the cause of it, so they made a fire of desert plants and burnt a piece of alum upon it before cooking their bread in its hot ashes. What they saw in the behaviour of the alum I do not know, but they said afterwards quite oracularly, "It is not our camels which have caused the *sitt* to be ill, but it was some jealous person who thought of her whilst she was crossing the Red Sea, and cast a spell over her that she cannot shake off." I replied that I never thought the camels were to blame, but that if they had understood better how to make my saddle comfortable there might have been no cause for burning alum. I was touched, however, by their ignorant solicitude about my welfare.

We photographed some of the numerous rock inscriptions

in the Wady Mukattab. These were regarded with intense interest some fifty years ago, before the late Professor Palmer, Dr. Euting, and others, had deciphered them. They were at first supposed to be the work of the Israelites, and to be a link in the chain of evidence which has been adduced to identify Serbal with the Mount of the Law, but it is now clearly proved that they were written by Nabathean traders in the fourth century. Dr. Euting, who has traversed most of the Sinai Peninsula on foot with extraordinary pluck, has lately made the humorous suggestion that they served the purpose of a hotel book, in which each traveller inserted his name as he passed a given place, sometimes at an interval of one or more years, and that this explains the frequent occurrence of the same name. The floor of these wadys is always seamed by the bed of a winter torrent, which has become a mosaic of many-coloured stones, from the pink granite of Sinai and the gray granite of Serbal to the white quartz and red sandstone of the district nearer the sea. As we gazed on the perfectly bare mountains, whose vivid hues lend such a charm to desert scenery, and noted the fantastic forms of the chalk cliffs and the dark ridges of trap-rock which seem to have broken through the granite, we wondered that any year passes over this region without its being traversed by some party of ardent geologists.

Mrs. Gibson had brought a little Frena kodak with her, while I had undertaken the very simple duty of replenishing it with films. I was doing so after dark in the Wady Solaf when a stupid little boy, named Hassan, set fire to a heap of sticks outside our tent, and spoiled twenty photographs. I suppose it was the nervousness produced in me by this accident which let to my putting in the next packet wrong, with the result that each time we took a picture a brown paper 'back' was presented to the lens instead of a film, and the Frena gave us next to no photographs in this the first year of its trial. It has since made ample amends for its failure (or rather mine).

Why should we have got a Frena, it may be asked, when we had already a good camera, and were accustomed to scientific photography? It was for the sake of taking groups and near objects out of doors. It requires time to put a camera up, with its tripod. More than once we have been greatly disappointed when, after proposing to take some picturesque party of Arabs who were squatting carelessly, displaying their bare limbs, on the sand, we came to focus them and found that they had made use of our preparation time in gathering their robes decently but prosaically about them, and otherwise posing.

An amusing story which illustrates this is current in Cambridge. One of our lady friends was taking part in the agitation for Home Rule. She went to Ireland to investigate matters for herself, and desiring to get evidence about the wretchedness into which Saxon tyranny had brought the people of a certain village, she sent a photographer down from Dublin to take a large group of them. What was her vexation, on receiving the photograph, to find that they had all put on their Sunday clothes, and looked as respectable as if they had come out of a Protestant church in the larger of the British Isles! A snapshot Kodak or Frena would have given her what she wanted, though from its small size and its uncertainty it would be, so far as I know, useless for manuscripts.

Mrs. Gibson sometimes remarked to the Arabs that the sun could not be a perfectly good Moslem, or he would not help us to take pictures. We did not find the Bedawîn so prejudiced on this point as some of our Egyptian friends, who have assured me that it is sinful to paint the likeness of anything in heaven or in earth; or as an old woman who tried to scratch Mrs. Gibson's eyes out when she pointed the Frena at a procession of Mohammedan pilgrims on their way to the tomb of Moses, not far from Jerusalem.

My sister thought that we had some illustrations in our daily life of Rebecca's action as described in Genesis xxiv, 64. We are told that on seeing Isaac she alighted from her camel, or rather, as the Hebrew has it, she "fell from her camel." This evidently means that she got off it suddenly, without waiting for the slow process of the driver coaxing it to kneel. The Bedawîn constantly drop down in this way, but it is hardly a safe action for a woman in flowing raiment.

CHAPTER III

OUR STAY AT THE CONVENT

ON SATURDAY, February 9th, we climbed the rocky pass of the Nugb Hawa, or Gap of the Wind, guided by Hassan, who made amends for the mischief he had done to our photographs by entertaining us with stories of a leopard hunt which he had witnessed there. The Nugb Hawa is one of the few entrances into the heart of the great block of pink granite mountains whose kernel is Sinai, and it leads directly into the vast plain called Er-Rahah, "The Rest," probably because the Israelites encamped there so long after their fight with the Amalekites in the Serbal district. The road was very rough, running betwixt rugged cliffs and amongst the huge boulders which are brought down, not so much by frost as by the "*seil*"★ or rushing torrent which carries all before it, when, after heavy rain, even of a few hours, the accumulated water, leaping from every mountain side, un-checked by vegetation, fills the valleys to the depth of six or ten feet in its headlong course towards the sea, and perhaps even more by the effect of intense solar heat splitting up the granite rocks. So powerful is this latter cause that many of the mountain-tops round Sinai are crowned by a large rock which looks just on the point of toppling over to lie beside its former neighbours

★ *Scottish* "spate."

in the valley beneath, and it is a never-ending source of interest to fit the fallen boulders into their ancient high places with the eye of the imagination. Four prolonged visits to the Wady-ed-Deir, or Valley of the Convent, have enabled us to observe that the cliffs of Jebel Mousa itself suffer a yearly change of contour. This was most clearly seen in the spring of 1895, when, standing on Aaron's Hill opposite the mouth of the little wady, we looked in vain for a crooked fissure on a cliff of the Râs Sufsafah which had, in 1893, as Dr. Rendel Harris pointed out, the distinct form of the Hebrew letter *lamed*.

The plain "Er-Rahah" is one of those features of the scenery which contribute powerfully to the identification of the Râs Sufsafah with the Mount of the Law. Major H. S. Palmer, of the Survey Expedition, has pointed how perfectly its rampart of granite mountains isolates it from the rest of the world. This is pierced only by the narrow defile of the Nugb Hawa, and by a more gentle ascent from the Wady-esh-Sheikh. As the sheer cliffs of the Râs Sufsafah burst on our view when we reached the top of the pass, we descended just a little into the sandy plain, and saw for ourselves not only the mount which might be touched, and had therefore to be fenced round, but the ample space afforded by the vast area before it, by the mouth of the Wady-esh-Sheikh, and by the slopes of the encircling mountains, for the accommodation of the multitudes who saw its smoke, and heard the voice of the Living God in thunder.

All this is unscientific, we shall be told. We cannot prove that the events recorded in the Exodus are not the amplification and embellishment in post-Mosaic times of a few simple historical facts. But it is curious how exactly the local features of the district suit with the sacred narrative. The claims of Mount Serbal to be Sinai are easily disposed of in the minds of those who have seen Er-Rahah, and that broadening of the Wady-esh-Sheikh, which is its rival, and is actually separated from Serbal by several miles of distance, and by the intervention of a range of low hills.

Robinson found the breadth of Er-Rahah to be in one place 2700 feet, and the length about 7000 feet. This gives a surface of nearly one square mile, and it is doubled if we include the opening of the Leja and that of Wady-esh-Sheikh, both of which command a perfect view of the mountain.

Captain H. S. Palmer gives the area of the plain as 400 acres; and that of the whole available space, including the mountain slopes, in full view of the Râs Sufsafah, as 940 acres.

Sinai is really a block of mountains 8550 feet in height. About 1600 feet from the top it branches upwards into three peaks, Jebel Catarina, Jebel Musa, which is considered by the monks to be the traditional Mount of the Law, and the Râs Sufsafah, or Mount of the Willow.

The scenery in these lonely valleys is almost too grand for description. Whether we gazed on the majestic rugged cliffs around us in the fierce glare of daylight as they stood out sharp against the intense blue of the sky, or watched the shadows creeping upwards on their worn sides when the sun had dipped behind Jebel Musa, one hour before his actual setting, and saw the vivid contrast of their summits bathed in golden radiance, as if the glory of Him Whose robe is the light touched them, or whether we stood in the garden in the clear moonlight, looking at the sheer towering cliffs and the tall waving cypresses, or at the carpet of fallen almond blossoms at our feet, with a glimmer on it as of snow, we felt how suitable the whole place is for the communion of man with his Maker.

We reached the Convent at 11.30, and were received by Father Eumenios, the new Economos, in Galaktéon's old room, which had been converted into the Economîa, or steward's room. There we had coffee, and afterwards lunch, and waited till our tents arrived. Galaktéon's office as Prior had not been filled up; the Archbishop being permanent Abbot, and having now been in residence for more than a year, there was no need for a second in command.

The many hints as to changes in the Convent which Father Nicodemus had given us in Cairo were more than justified. It fell to my lot that day, as it does to that of few people, to see the fulfilment of an object on which I had once set my heart, and for which I had made a little effort to raise funds, realised by other means. We could already see from the outside of the library that it had undergone renovation, and there was also a new substantial whitewashed building, whose upper floor, with its five large sunny windows, had been reared for the convenience of European students. It occupies the highest position in the Convent, so as to catch all possible light, and what amused me very much is that the staircase leading to the platform on which it stands is a way by which most of the monks must pass from their cells to the church. They have thus their foreign visitors, while engaged with the manuscripts, under quite as effectual observation as the officials of the British Museum have their readers. And who that has seen books composed of illuminated frontispieces and title-pages of ancient manuscripts, or who that considers how a well-known leaf of the Codex Ephremi in Paris is now missing, shall say that this is not necessary and proper?

I must here explain that the monks of the Sinai Convent, before the visit of Messrs. Rendel Harris and Bliss, in 1889, had shown great distrust of European scholars, and had been unwilling to allow all their treasures to be examined. The irritation produced by the loss of the Codex Sinaiticus, which Tischendorf carried off on loan to the Emperor of Russia, and then, after the lapse of ten years, persuaded a young Archbishop to make a gift (or perhaps a sale) of to his imperial patron was still fresh in their minds, and so were the unkind comments on this transaction made by the Press of Europe. Moreover, it is, perhaps, a habit of some learned men who visit Eastern monasteries to do so with a single eye to their own profit, and to show this perhaps a little too plainly; by giving the monks no information, either about their own work or about the value of their MSS; to treat them, in fact, as if they were the hopelessly stupid people which some travellers assume them to be. That this cause of trouble is not quite imaginary may be illustrated by the story which we heard in Cairo about the doings of a certain young Englishman, who went into a Coptic church and threatened the terrified priests with the vengeance of the British Government because they declined to sell a beautifully-worked silver censer to which he had taken a fancy.

I cannot help thinking that one of our own countrymen, who had come into an inheritance of ancient coins and other objects which his education enabled him to appreciate only in a vague way, and who permitted a couple of experts to examine these, would behave in precisely the same fashion as the monks have done if he found that one of these gentlemen took copious notes for publication, treating the owner of the treasure merely as a person bound to provide him with coffee and stationery, and left without vouchsafing a word of explanation about anything he had examined. If he found the other full of human sympathy, and ready to communicate all that he wanted to know, so that without any great learning he might yet feel a genuine delight in his own property, it would only be natural for him to unlock all his secret cupboards and bring their contents under the eyes of his more generous visitor. I am far from saying that all travellers to Sinai before 1889 behaved as I have pictured No. I., but the faults of others were certainly visited on Niebuhr, who in A.D. 1762 was refused admittance to the convent for lack of a letter from its Cairo branch; on Schimper, who in A.D. 1835 on approaching with a large Bedawîn escort was greeted with a shower of stones; and on Professor Palmer, of Cambridge, to whom in 1869 the monks seem to have shown more than one Syriac palimpsest, lying, probably, in the very box where the Gospels were found, but whose attempt to catalogue the Arabic manuscripts was frustrated by the many hindrances placed in his way.*

The men who went there in A.D. 1889 followed a wiser course. To them the formidable barrier of language had no existence. Dr. Bliss spoke Arabic like a native of Syria, and Dr. Rendel Harris read modern Greek, whilst both had that kind genial manner which disarms suspicion, and the ready tact which has proved so effective in the case of the one who has since tracked nearly 2500 feet of the old wall of Jerusalem beneath the property of a host of recalcitrant natives. My sister and I entered fully into the inheritance of the reputation they had left behind them.

More than once I have been informed, somewhat to my surprise, by Cambridge friends, that we have learnt the Greek language "from the modern side." We have adopted, it is true, the modern Athenian pronunciation, with due regard to accents, but we began with the Eton Greek grammar, passing on to the German Greek one of George Curtius, and then studied the ancient poets, dramatists, and historians for three years before we took up modern Greek as an adjunct to our travels. The monks were greatly amused by the archaisms which we employed in conversing with them.

We told Father Euthymios that we did not wish to begin working in the library until we had had an interview with the Archbishop, and had explained our views to him. There were then 100 pilgrims lodged in the Convent. His Grace's time and that of the very active Euthymios was completely occupied with them, so we saw that it would be impossible for us to have this interview until Monday.

But what a change had taken place in the Convent! It was not only that of a new building, but everything had become very clean and orderly. Poor Galaktéon, with his many virtues, was

* *Desert of the Exodus*, p. 68.

not the pink of perfection in this respect, and the air of tidiness which now reigned in his old apartments would hardly have suited him. A whitewash brush had passed all over the building, and there were only two things left for us to regret, the disappearance of the old but substantial bench on which we had often sat awaiting Galaktéon's advent with the keys, and the casing of the very thick and very ancient entrance doors with modern sheet iron painted blue. I remarked to Father Euthymios that this had an incongruous effect, and was met by the query so common in Greece, Τι να καμωμεν ("What can we do?"). It was evident, however, that an orderly and cultivated mind had now taken the supreme direction of things.

Our tents were in the process of being pitched, and I was supplying our liberated fowls with water, when I was startled by a most unearthly roar, again and again repeated. I rushed to the shed outside the garden gate, and here I found about a dozen Bedawîn holding down a poor camel on its back, whilst one of them applied a burning hot iron to its thigh, with the aid of a charcoal brazier. I was greatly distressed, but in answer to my remonstrances I was told that this was their medicine, that it was applied to growths (probably boils) on the camel, which would otherwise be slow to heal. "Well," I said, "if such a cruel operation was necessary, why did you not let the poor creature have a few minutes' time to breathe and rest after its journey? You seized it for this purpose the moment after it had got its load off, when it ought to have been enjoying food and water." There are few camels who do not bear marks of having undergone this treatment at some period of their lives, often more than once. I have been told by a British officer that the men of our Camel corps in Egypt use a lotion for these growths which is both more efficacious and more humane.

The party of monks who had travelled by way of Tor arrived before us, and on both Saturday and Sunday we had them to tea in our tents, with much pleasant conversation.

On Sunday we found every exit from the Convent closed, so we had to confine our walk to the lower terraces of the garden, where some of the monks came and talked to us, giving us handfuls of almonds. I always regret that I have never brought home any of their vegetable seeds.

From ten to twelve o'clock we watched the pilgrims departing. The outer gate of the courtyard was kept locked, and was opened only to admit the entry of one batch of camels as another departed. One camel was allotted to every two of the pilgrims, and on it they piled their very miscellaneous chattels, bundles of clothing, pans, kettles, pillows, palm branches etc. The women were mostly sturdy and elderly, though there were a few young ones. Their clothing was of round homespun, suitable for a cold climate, and they displayed admirable patience whilst awaiting their turn to be attended to. The men, rather fewer in number, had many of them shock heads of hair and long beards. The expression of their faces betokened great simplicity, not to say stupidity and good nature. The mixture of heavy Slavonian faces with those of the lithe dusky Bedawîn, and the pale clear-cut and occasionally classic features of the dark-robed monks was not a little remarkable. These poor people do the desert journey, and also that through Palestine, entirely on foot, sleeping frequently in the open air. In 1893 about seventy of those whom we had met at Sinai perished of cold and exposure during heavy rains in the plain of Esdraelon. There had been some dispute between the Russian priests, guides of the pilgrimage, and the Greek Convents about the price paid for their accommodation, and the former had attempted without success to provide what was requisite. It is said that some of the pilgrims did not even try to seek shelter, but lay down on the wet ground and drank till they were unconscious. We believe that an arrangement has been made by which this is not likely to happen a second time.

The Archbishop stood at the door of the Convent, giving his

parting blessing to all who sought it. He gave us a cordial welcome, and made many apologies for being unable to receive a visit from us till the pilgrims should have departed. The monks flitted amongst the crowd, and even the most boyish of them was continually stopped and asked for a benediction. Some Russian priests there were, but neither in dress nor in demeanour were they to be distinguished from their peasant flock.

Next morning we contrived to get the outer gate of the Convent opened by negotiations with the Arab *bawwab*, or porter. The monks spent the morning in solemn conclave with closed doors. The Archbishop sent for us at about half-past four, receiving us in the little room which he was occupying at the end of the visitors' gallery. Everything in it was a pattern of neatness, in strong contrast to the picturesque old traditions of the Convent. We found that through some vagary of the Post-Office his Grace had not received the two volumes of the "Syriac Gospels as transcribed from the Sinaitic Palimpsest," which had been sent to him by the Syndics of the Cambridge University Press. Our copy was therefore the first he had seen, and he turned over its leaves with the greatest possible interest. "What a pity there are so many gaps in the text," was one of his first remarks. "These are what we have come to try and fill up," I replied, "if you will let us have the manuscript to work at." "Yes, you will have every facility," he responded. We then had a lively discussion about some of the remarkable readings in the Codex, and obtained his Grace's permission not only to use the re-agent where we found it necessary, but also to number its pages and those of any other manuscript we might wish to read. This effected a great saving of our time in finding places, as the pages are all so accurately marked in the published edition.

We went for our evening walk, and lingered on the plain of Er Rahah, quite oblivious of our being in a land where no twilight precedes the fall of darkness. We had re-entered the valley, when we suddenly found that we could hardly see a step before us. We raced on as fast as we could, the great rocks that fringed the path looming like ghosts in the darkness, and only got in with the help of a lantern brought by one of our servants. Father Eumenios was standing within the gate of the courtyard, key in hand, and he gave us the scolding we deserved—first for having exposed ourselves to danger, and secondly for having obliged him to relax a monastic rule by keeping the gate open for us.

Our walks were usually down the valley, along the dilapidated road made by Abbas Pasha, but always over rough stones or the gravel of broken granite, which made great havoc of both shoes and stockings. The pink rock of Sinai, so we were told by Mr. Wiles, the Cambridge sculptor, is harder to cut or to polish than that of either Peterhead or Aberdeen. We may assume that it is the hardest in the world. Yet we are told that there was not a weary nor a foot-sore person amongst all the tribes of Israel. At the mouth of the little wady are the remains of a modern stone encampment, which once sheltered Abbas' troops, and there is a Bedawy cemetery in the sand. Mohammed, our quondam sheikh* accompanied us thither, and, pointing to the little white stones which mark the graves, said, "My father was buried here, but the hyenas came and took the body away." "You did not dig the grave deep enough," we said. "Yes I did, but however deep you make it, the hyena tunnels from a distance, where you cannot find it out, and gets at the body." Mrs. Gibson thereupon drew our attention to the biting sarcasm of the taunt flung at Moses by his rebellious flock: "Because there were no graves in Egypt, hast thou taken us away to die in the wilderness†?" The rock-hewn tombs which fill so large a part of the Nile valley have been quite as powerless as the desert sand to protect their occupants.

* He had lost his camel in 1893, and was glad to be engaged by Ahmed and Joseph as scullion.
† Exodus xiv, 11.

CHAPTER IV

THE PALIMPSEST

ON TUESDAY morning we went into the library, escorted by Father Euthymios and others. Mounting by the old steep staircase to the so-called Archbishop's room, in which so much of our work in former years had been done, we found that doors on either side of it opened into two lofty spacious rooms fitted with bookshelves of plain unpolished wood, on which were ranged all the MSS in order, the Greek ones according to the elaborate manuscript catalogue possessed by the monks, which they have never printed, and the Gardhausen's somewhat bald epitome of the same; the Semitic ones according to the rather rough catalogues which we drew up in 1893. "What book do you want first?" asked Euthymios. "No. 30," I replied, "the book that the three gentlemen worked so constantly on two years ago." Euthymios planted his ladder against the shelves and made diligent search. "It is not there," he said, "we haven't got it."

The reader may imagine our blank disappointment. I knew too well that our Oxford friends had not seen it in 1894, and I feared that it might have been disposed of by some secret negotiation.

"The Archbishop told us last night that it *is* there," I insisted, "and that we were to have full liberty to copy it. What have you done with the box I sent you from England to keep it in?" "The box?" cried Euthymios, "but I don't know where that is either. I have not seen it for a long time."

I sat down in great discouragement, and what the French so aptly call "a bad quarter-of-an-hour." Euthymios disappeared, and I was indulging in the most gloomy reflections when my sister's voice roused me: "Agnes, there it is!" she cried, "It's coming!" I looked up and saw not the palimpsest, but the stripes of the silk cover, which Mrs. Bensly had bestowed on it, in Euthymios' hands. "It was in the box," he said, "but that had been locked away, and I forgot all about it." And evidently it had not been lately handled, for the transcribers' marks were there exactly where we would expect to find them, little strips of Cambridge blue riband and of paper, some at the division between the portions allotted to each of our friends, some at remarkable passages, such as the end of St. Mark's Gospel. We were very glad to know that we were not to work in the library, but in the new students' room, which was both sunny and warm.

We had agreed that Mrs. Gibson was to share with me the work of the supplementary decipherment, but she unfortunately began with an almost impossible page containing Matt. xxv, 13–25. Moreover, her eyes had not grown accustomed to the character of the text as mine had done, through constant study of the photographs; and thus the slope of the writing was a puzzle to her. She therefore confined herself to finding all the passages about which Dr. Rendel Harris, Mr. Burkitt, and others had expressed doubts, and trying with my assistance to verify them.

I of course made some use of the re-agent. This takes time, for one has to apply it very cautiously to a palimpsest, so as not to make the ink of the upper-writing run. It had to be used within the four walls of a room instead of as formerly in the open air, and it served the useful purpose of shortening the visits of the curious, whether monks or others. After the first bottle was uncorked our leisure became ample.

I worked for four hours that day and copied 133 words, or less than three pages; next day I worked for six hours and copied 137 words. In the first twelve days I copied 800 words or 16 pages, working about seven hours a day, so it is evident that I took the less difficult passages first, working ever more and more slowly. The blanks which I was trying to fill up were scattered over the whole text, so that most of what I did linked the sense of it together. It was delightful to find out that I could see to do it all with the constant help of a magnifying glass. And I got so accustomed to the scent from my bottle, that I actually came to like it. Mrs. Gibson, however, was completely upset on one occasion when she had opened a second bottle in the room for some work of her own, I believe it was to look at the very difficult triple palimpsest transcribed by Mr. Stenning, and published in *Anecdota Oxoniensia,* Vol. I, Part IX.

The palimpsest is now almost without a cover, the old one having dropped off piecemeal. Only a triangular fragment remains, firmly fixed to f.1, which the binding formerly enclosed. This accounts for the gap there visible in Dr. Harris' transcription (Matt. xiv, 14, 15, 21–23). I dare not loosen it for fear of doing damage, but on the other hand, I was delighted when my sister pointed out to me that f.1 is not a palimpsest; that we have in it a specimen of what the pages were originally like before John of Beth Mari covered them over with his stories of women saints, Thekla, Eugenia, Euphrosyne, and others. Portions have crumbled away from the margins of the first four leaves, and with them has gone the name of John Beth Mari himself, but it is preserved in one of my photographs.

When we left Sinai in 1893, Professor Bensly had copied, working by himself, what would fill, if placed together, about 27 pages. Mr. Burkitt had done by himself, inclusive of the pages he had copied from my photographs before leaving home, nearly 69 pages, Professor Bensly and Mr. Burkitt, working together, 27 pages, and Dr. Rendel Harris 100¼ pages. Mr. Burkitt afterwards added to this 18½ pages from my fresh photographs, so that there remained a portion amounting to about 42 pages still to do. By filling up the numerous *lacunae*, and copying a very few whole pages, I reduced these 42 to 6½. I also compared every word of the transcription already published with the text of the manuscript. No one who knows what a palimpsest is can wonder that a few corrections had to be made in this; and I was glad that all my three friends had been enabled to give their skill to it, for if any one of them had stayed away we should have been the poorer by the amount of his work, or rather the amount of that work would have been transferred to my supplementary volume, seeing that all three did their very utmost in the time at their disposal. Professor Bensly and Mr. Burkitt revised some of each other's work at Sinai, but a one-sided revision only was proposed to Dr. Harris, and he preferred, with my cordial approval, to reserve this for Professor Bensly's eyes until after his return to Cambridge. Providence willed that this revision should not take place, and the duty devolved on the Rev. R. H. Kennett, who succeeded Professor Bensly in the Syriac chair, and who also read over the proofs of the whole text.

The piece of my work on that occasion which has given me the greatest satisfaction consists in the decipherment of two words in John iv. 27. They were well worth all our visits to Sinai, for they illustrate an action of our Lord which seems to be recorded nowhere else, and which has some degree of inherent probability from what we know of His character. The passage is, "His disciples came and wondered that with the woman He was *standing and talking*." Professor Bensly had seen the final letter of the word *qaem,* "standing," and, not being able to guess what it was, he had conjectured the letter *l* before it, thus making the unimportant particle *lam*. I saw at the first glance that there was no *l*, and that a little brown *Alaf a* was embedded in a word of the upper-writing. I did not touch this, but a light application of my brush brought up a *q* before that again so as to form the word *qaem. E* is one of those short vowels which are not written in ancient Syriac.

Why was our Lord standing? He had been sitting on the well when the disciples left Him, and we know that He was tired. Moreover, sitting is the proper attitude for an Eastern when engaged in teaching. And an ordinary Oriental would never rise of his own natural free will out of politeness to a woman. It may be that He rose in His enthusiasm for the great truths he was uttering, but I like to think that His great heart, which embraced the lowest of humanity, lifted Him above the restrictions of His race and age, and made Him show that courtesy to our sex, even in the person of a degraded specimen, which is considered amongst all really progressive persons to be a mark of true and noble manhood. To shed even a faint light upon that wondrous story of His tabernacling amongst us, is an inestimable privilege, and worth all the trouble that we can possibly take.

Many other readings of this Gospel text are very valuable, and there are not a few which confirm the judgment of the New Testament revisers, although in Luke ii, 14 we have the old version of "good will to men." Some carry their own recommendation in themselves by giving a more natural sense than that of readings hitherto accepted. Such are:

Mark x, 49, 50 concerning Timai-Bar-Timai. "And they said unto him, Fear not, rise, He calleth thee. And he rose, and took up his garment, and came to Jesus."

That he took up his garment is more in accordance with Oriental habits than if he had cast it away, he being about to appear in the presence of a superior, and under the eyes of a crowd.

Mark xvi, 3,4. "And they said among themselves, But who shall roll us away the stone of the sepulchre? for it was very great. And they went, and saw that this stone was rolled away."

A similar reading occurs in Codex Bezae and in the Gospel of

Pseudo-Peter, c. 12. The explanation "for it was very great" comes more naturally in the description of the women's thoughts than where it occurs in most of the Greek MSS of St. Mark after the statement that the stone was rolled back.

Luke i, 63, 64. "And he asked for a writing tablet, and wrote on it, John is his name. And straightway the string of his tongue was loosened, and he blessed God. And they all wondered."

It is here implied that the cause of the people's wonder was the loosening of Zacharias' tongue rather than his writing of the name "John."

Luke vii, 29. "And all the people and the publicans that heard [Him] justified themselves to God,* who were baptized with the baptism of John."

John vii, 56, 57. "Abraham was longing to see My day; and he saw and was glad. The Jews say unto Him, Thou art not fifty years old, and hath Abraham seen Thee?"

This reading is also found in the Codex Sinaiticus, and I am indebted to my friend Mr. Theodore Harris for pointing out that the Codex Vaticanus appears at this point to have been tampered with. It had originally εορακεσε but the final ε has been erased, and the ε preceding it changed into α. "Hath Abraham seen Thee?" was surely a more probable question for the Jews to ask our Lord after His own statement than "Hast Thou seen Abraham?"

John vi, 29, 30. "His disciples said unto Him, Lo, now also speakest thou plainly, and speakest no parable at all unto us, now we know that Thou knowest all things, and needest not that Thou shouldest ask any man, by this we believe that Thou art sent from God." This is surely better than "needest not that any man should ask Thee."

The most startling and remarkable of its variants, that in Matt. i, 16 was quite unknown to me while we were at Sinai, and I

---

* Not "justified God."

became aware of it only some weeks after our return, through a letter from Mrs. Humphry Ward. Mr. Kennett, afterwards in September, told me the exact words: "Joseph to whom was betrothed Mary the Virgin, begat Jesus, who is called the Christ."

I was at first greatly shocked, and was tempted to regret that I had unearthed such an heretical document. But a long course of meditation on the subject, assisted by the discussion which took place in the columns of the *Academy* from Nov. 17th, 1894, till Feb. 23rd, 1895, led me to see that the phrase is only the natural corollary to an official register of successions rather than of actual descents; witness the statements that Joram begat his grandson Ozias, and that childless Jeconiah begat his nephew Salathiel. It does not stamp our Codex as heretical any more than the phrase uttered by the thrice blessed mother of our Lord, "Thy father and I have sought Thee sorrowing," stamps in a similar way all the great Greek codices.

A very interesting light is thrown on our Lord's social position as the supposed son of Joseph, by a statement in Dr. Robertson Smith's interesting book *Kinship and Marriage in Early Arabia*. I quote his words, leaving his readers to make the application for themselves.

"I now proceed to show that the Arab idea of paternity is strictly correlated to the conception just developed of the nature of the contract of marriage by purchase. A man is father of all the children of the woman by whom he has purchased the right to have offspring that shall be reckoned to be his own kin. This, as is well known, is the fundamental doctrine of Mohammedan law, *el-walad lil firash*, the son is reckoned to the bed on which he is born." p. 109.

Again: "Ultimately if a child is born in the tribe of a woman brought in by contract of marriage, it was reckoned to the tribal stock as a matter of course without enquiry as to its natural procreator." p. 120.

Again: "As there was no difference between an adopted and a real son before Islam, emancipated slaves appear in the genealogical lists without any note of explanation, just as if they had been pure Arabs." p. 45.

The early Arabs were not Hebrews, it is true, but they and the Hebrews were descended from a common ancestor, and their habits show the trend of Semitic thought.

With the exception of three verses, Matt. i, 16, 21, 25, I feel safe in affirming that no charge of heresy can be successfully brought against any part of our Codex. The expression, "chosen" with reference to our Lord occurs twice in our English versions (Matt. xii, 18; Luke xxiii, 35), and "my beloved" twice in the Sinai palimpsest (Mark ix, 7; Luke iii, 22).

It may be said, on behalf of the Old Syriac version, that in both the Sinai MS and the Cureton we find the word "wife" in place of the doubtful εμυηστευμεη which Drs. Westcott and Hort have been obliged by the Greek MSS to adopt in Luke ii, 5, and which the Revisers have translated "who was betrothed to him," and the Authorised translators, "espoused wife," the Peshitta having simply "espoused." Mary, according to the earlier Syrians, was "espoused," or "betrothed," before she was visited by the angel, and before she saluted Elizabeth, and returned to her own house. But she was under the full legal protection of Joseph, was undoubtedly his wife when she travelled with him to Bethlehem, and gave birth to her Divine Son. Do not the Syrians, therefore, give us clearer ideas about her whom all generations call blessed, and is this a slight gain?

The *Church Quarterly Review* for April, 1895, contained a very able and ingenious article on the subject of the Sinai palimpsest, which was, nevertheless, written without a full knowledge of all the facts. The reviewer supposed that certain passages had been erased from the manuscript by the monks of a later age because they were unsound on the question of our Lord's divinity. I am not ungrateful for the eulogy which has bestowed on me personally, but, nevertheless, I am obliged to point out that at the very time he was writing I was on my way from Sinai to Cambridge, bringing with me another precious transcript, a transcript of some of those very passages on whose supposed obliteration from the manuscript his charge of heresy was partly founded. Moreover, it did not occur to him that if John the Recluse, or any other orthodox believer, had sat down deliberately to expunge the offending passages in a heretical manuscript, he would surely have begun with Matt. i, 16. Yet the page which contains that verse is one of the clearest and best preserved in the whole of the palimpsest. Surely we are not going to shut our eyes for its sake to the beautiful picture of our Lord standing while He spoke to the degraded woman of Samaria, nor to the graphic touches in the account of His burial by loving, timid hands in John xix, 42: "And hastily, suddenly, they laid Him in the new* sepulchre which was nigh at hand, because the sabbath was dawning."

Nor can we willingly overlook the improved arrangement in the story of our Lord's trial in John xviii., where by the transposition of *v*. 24 to a place betwixt *v*. 13 and *v*. 14, and of *vv*. 16, 17, 18 to one betwixt *v*. 23 and *v*. 25, greater consistency is given to the narrative, and a seeming discrepancy between St. John and the Synoptic Evangelists is removed, for St. John also states that the trial took place in the house of Caiaphas, and not in that of Annas.† And here I must say, that I, for one, cannot see the cogency of the argument which is sometimes urged against the Virgin-birth from the silence about it of the Acts and the Epistles.‡ Paul, Luke, James and Peter were shrewd, practical men of the world, who were not likely to make a fact, which by its very nature was not susceptible of proof, the pivot of their reasoning. Not the virgin-birth, but the Resurrection was the mast to which they nailed their colours. Believe that, and all the other miracles will seem to you in the highest degree probable; disprove it, and human life is again

---

* The word "new" was read by me in 1897.
† See Dr. Blass' *Philology of the Gospels,* pp. 56–9.
‡ See H. R. Haweis in the *Contemporary Review* for October, 1895, p. 600.

overhung by the dark impenetrable cloud of the shadow of death.

To this question, we rejoice to say, the Sinai palimpsest gives no equivocal answer.

CHAPTER V

PRAYERS FOR RAIN

THE ARCHBISHOP remained in residence for about ten days after our arrival. We had very violent winds, and it was a question as to whether His Grace or we were the most incommoded by them. As our tents were tied to olive trees, we felt tolerably secure at night, and fairly warm, though icicles were frequently hanging from our earthenware water-bottle, which had been suspended on the branch of a tree outside. The Archbishop took a great interest in our work, visiting us in the students' room occasionally, although we had made the atmosphere there none too sweet for an outsider. His departure for Tor was accompanied by the ringing of bells, beating of the iron gong and the wooden gong in the church tower, and the firing of cannon from the battlements, which continued until after he and his beautiful white donkey had disappeared from sight on the path up the Wady ed Deir. An impressive ceremony had previously taken place outside the inner doors of the Convent, when the monks knelt by turns to receive his blessing.

A few days afterwards we were present at a service in the church, in celebration of the Archbishop's name-day. The prayers chanted for him were very interesting. He was spoken of in a particular fashion. A bunch of the huge Convent keys was laid before his empty throne during part of the service, and was again removed with great ceremony, I suppose in symbolical acknowledgement of His Grace's rights as Hegoumenos.

Galaktéon's name was also recited first of all in the prayer of thanksgiving for those departed this life.

The singing was very fine and impressive, every word being distinctly heard. The monks repeat their liturgy no less than eight times in the twenty-four hours, each being expected to assist with it at least twice during the day, and twice during the night. These vigils necessitate a certain amount of rest in the day-time, and they are forgotten by those superficial observers who accuse our friends of laziness.

The inhabitants of the Sinai peninsula were at that time almost at their wits' end as to how they could obtain water for their camels and their flocks. Nothing less than a famine was threatened, for not a drop of water had fallen since March or April of the previous year—in fact, since the flood of which our young Oxford friends, Messrs. Cowley and Stenning, were witnesses. This had been only too evident during our journey from Suez. The tor-trees at Ghurundel and the palms at Feirân had all looked miserable; there was hardly a plant alive in the Convent valley; the olives and almond-trees in the garden were drooping; and the fine old cypresses had dropped their leaves, so as to resemble scaffolding poles. The monks lamented the lowness of the water in their wells, and one morning we were surprised by the arrival of three sheikhs, who had come a long four days' journey as a deputation from the tribes of the Tih, for the purpose of requesting the monks to pray for rain. This was sufficiently remarkable as between Moslem and Christian,★ but still more curious was it when they preferred a like request to our dragoman. "But it will be of no use," they said, "unless you put on a white dress and go to the top of Jebel Musa about midnight,

★ The Bedawîn firmly believe that the monks possess the two Tables of the Law, written by Moses, either built into the wall of the Chapel of the Burning bush, or concealed in the ruins of the church on the top of Jebel Musa.

and pray there." Joseph excused himself by saying that the great thing was for people to pray for themselves. "If you don't do that," he said, "my prayers won't help you much." When we spoke to the monks of the drought they always said, "It is for our sins."

It will be readily understood that in these circumstances the face of the sky was to us a never-failing source of eager interest; especially in the afternoons. Every cloud we saw sailing above the summit of the Râs Sufsafaha, or gathering over our own valley towards sunset, we earnestly hoped might grow and give us the coveted blessing. One night the sky became perfectly covered; dark masses of cloud hung lower and lower, till when we sat down to dinner we expected every moment to hear the plash of rain. Joseph had dug trenches all round our tents, and, I think, as we were changing our photographic films after dark we actually did hear a sound like that of drops. But when we rose next morning the sky was as blue as a sapphire, and the sand as dry as the ashes in an English grate.

Father Eumenios, who, as Economos, was performing the duties of Hegoumenos in the Archbishop's absence, declared his conviction that there would now be no rain, as it was the season of summer. Mrs. Gibson told him that he had less faith in the efficacy of his own prayers than our dragoman had, as witness the trenches. The deputation of sheikhs departed, and for three weeks more the sky gave no sign of relenting.

The letters which reached us about that time were full of complaints about a scarcity of water in England, caused by frozen pipes. The columns of the *Times*, then a month old, were curious reading for us at Sinai.

The even tenor of our lives was at length broken by the arrival of other travellers. First came two young Germans, one of whom was named Wolf, and who thus verified a prediction of Father Eumenios. One night we were awakened by the shrieks of our poultry, and the scream of a poor fowl, which was evidently in its death-struggle. The coops were shifted next evening, and placed between the kitchen tent and ours, and round them was piled a barricade of boxes and tin saucepans.

The fowls screamed again after midnight, and Joseph awoke in time to see the yellow glaring eyes of a wild cat. Father Eumenios evinced no sympathy with us for the loss of several fowls—he said, "The cat must live, poor thing; it was hungry." The following night our coops were transferred to a stone hut, used by the Bedawy gardener, and great was our amusement next morning to hear that the robber, baulked of her feast on our poultry, had attacked that of the monks, and had left only one chicken alive. Father Eumenios was very reticent on the subject, but Euthymios owned to the catastrophe. The former tried to persuade us to reside in the Convent, as the wind was then at its highest, saying that if we persisted in sleeping in our tents we should next have a visit from a wolf.

The next arrivals were the Hon. and Mrs. Whitelaw Reid, who encamped in the garden terrace immediately above us. Mr. Reid had represented his country, the United States, as Ambassador to Great Britain for the Jubilee of our beloved Queen. He was then in delicate health, and they had travelled by very easy stages. We greatly enjoyed their society during the five days they spent at the Convent, and also later, during our voyage in the same steamer from Beyrout to Marseilles. They had both seen much of the world, and of royal circles, and as they were keen observers, their conversation was as instructive as it was agreeable. They were received by Father Eumenios, and we sat under the trees and translated for them whilst their tents were being prepared.

The only mishap that had occurred in their journey was the fall of Mr. Reid's English valet from his camel into the sea whilst it was wading past the rocks which impede the path near the spot where the Israelites camped. This was due to the carelessness of the sheikh, who had not provided sufficient men to lead the

camels of the party, and who accordingly received less in the way
of a present in tobacco from the dragoman than he would otherwise have done. No bones were broken, but it would have been
serious in the case of a traveller who could not swim, and I could
not help recollecting that in 1893 we had had one camel leader
too little for the most of our journey. So, although the sheikh
begged both Father Eumenios and ourselves to intercede for his
restoration to Mr. Reid's favour, I was heartily glad that the
Bedawîn had received a lesson about their duties.

Next came an English party of six, who encamped at the
mouth of the valley. Mrs. Gibson and I proposed to try the novel
experiment of giving a garden party at Sinai. We planned to have
little tables beneath the olive trees, with a display of cakes, sweets,
and fruits, which should be more remarkable for its elegant
simplicity than its luxuriance, and our guests were to be of three
nationalities, American, Greek, and English, waited on by
Syrian, Arabian, and Egyptian servants. The invitations met with
a ready acceptance. Our cook busied himself for three days in
baking a variety of cakes in an impromptu oven of loose stones
with an arched top, constructed by himself and by Joseph in the
open air. He could procure neither yeast nor baking powder
to make them rise, but they made a gallant show, and we
even concocted an imaginary paragraph to be inserted in the
fashionable intelligence of the *Sphinx* or the *Egyptian Gazette*,
descriptive of our festivity. The paragraph was never sent, for
two events happened which deprived the party of its promised
lustre.

The first was the departure of Mr. and Mrs. Whitelaw Reid
for Jerusalem, viâ Nekb, on Saturday morning. The second was
announced to me by the sudden clamour of the Convent bells
and gongs whilst I was engrossed in my transcription from the
palimpsest. I had noticed that the light was less brilliant than
usual, and on opening the door to see what might be the cause
of the commotion, I found that the flagstones were actually wet

with rain. That for which so many prayers had been offered was at length come, and in view of the unspeakable blessing which it was sure to bring to the whole country, we could not grieve over our very insignificant disappointment. We despatched a Bedawy down to the foot of the valley to beg our English friends not to come, and we ourselves told Father Eumenios that our reception could not be held. It takes more than a shower, however, to daunt the spirit of Britons; three of the party came in waterproofs and were amazed at the wonderful versatility of our cook. It was well that Father Eumenios and a party of monks appeared just as they were leaving, for if all had arrived together, we should not have had room for them in our little dripping tent.

The rain lasted for only a night, and it was followed by a sort of mistral, which blew both sand and small stones so violently about that for several days we could hardly venture out of the Convent gate without risk of being blinded. One evening when there was a lull, Mrs. Gibson ventured a little way up the valley. She returned after the inner gate had been shut, and heard someone shout to her from a high battlement. Looking up she saw Father Eumenios waving a newspaper. He let it drop, but ere it reached the ground the wind caught it and she had to chase it over the rocks. It contained the translation into Greek of a notice about her Catalogue of Arabic MS in the Convent library, which had appeared in the London *Athenæm*. Little did the writer of that notice imagine that a copy of it would be blown by the wind from the top of St. Catherine's Convent to the feet of the woman whose book he was reviewing.

Owing to a mistake in my calculations, I had brought very tiny bottles of the re-agent, less than a fourth of what I had actually used in 1893. The time came when I could decipher no more without a fresh supply. Father Euthymios and the English visitors both said I ought not to hesitate a moment in despatching a Bedawy and his camel to Suez to procure this. Joseph undertook to give the man proper instructions, and insisted particularly that he should return with the chemical in ten days. He also took advantage of the opportunity to procure some lettuce and other delicacies for our table. To guard against any possible mistake, I wrote a letter in Greek to the apothecary, and another in English to our vice-consul, who was so kindly taking charge of our letters. The man went and came back some twelve hours before the time appointed. He brought the lettuce, and a letter from the apothecary, stating that having no hydro-sulphuret of ammonia in stock, he had sent to Alexandria to have it made, and he hoped to send it on in a few days with some chance caravan. The Vice-Consul had sent our messenger to the English Hospital, where my letter had caused quite a flutter, for such a drug had never before been asked for in that quarter. Our young friends, Dr. Cresswell and Dr. Attfield, understood the situation, and they proposed to manufacture the article themselves; but alas! after they had come to that conclusion, the messenger was already crossing the sands about Hamman Far'aôn. Necessity, however, is the mother of invention, and I bethought me of a bottle which I had left with Father Galaktéon in 1893 for a keepsake. Though tightly corked and sealed, its contents had partly evaporated when Father Euthymios produced it triumphantly from the Convent stores. It contained more than I required.

We left Sinai on March 14th. Father Eumenios bade us farewell at the outer gate, expressing a fervent wish that we might reach our home in safety, with the blessing of the Almighty and of St. Catherine. An old monk came running after us to present us with some little pots of manna.

Our return as far as Wady Ghurundel was comfortably made, except that one of the journeys was rather long for our strength, that from a place in Wady-esh-Sheigh to Wady Sheikh Ahmed, beyond the Wady Bark, a distance of about twenty-seven miles. We thoroughly enjoyed our Sunday's rest in the Wady Nasb, which is a little off the usual route and contains one of the finest springs of water in the peninsula. We walked thither after breakfast, and it was most interesting to see the troops of camels which came to be watered from what looked like a mere hole in the ground. In the afternoon I wrote a letter to the *Academy*, which afterwards appeared on April 16th, giving an account of the fresh transcription which I had made from the palimpsest Gospels. I hoped by this means to give due warning to all who were engaged in critical work on its text, but unfortunately some of them failed to notice it.

We reached Ghurundel about noon on Monday, and dug up our buried water-bottles. I was not particularly happy, for I was suffering from a carbuncle. I could not count on the Bedawîn carrying me, for they are accustomed to put everything on their camels, and I did not know if a *tahterawan* could be procured in Suez. On the last day I walked for fifteen miles, and felt very miserable when we were deposited in the felucca. Joseph's whole thoughts were centred on how he was to take us to Mar Din in Mesapotamia, whilst mine were how I should get into a comfortable bed.

We sent for Dr. Cresswell that evening, and I remained under his care for two weeks. A terrific storm raged all night, making us glad to be away from our tents. It uprooted trees, knocked down houses, and banged the boltless door of my bedroom in a most distracting way. We parted with Joseph, and he returned his native village in the Lebanon, for it was evident that I must give up all thoughts of Mar Din. I had nothing beyond my mosquito curtains to look at for the next fortnight, whilst Mrs. Gibson distributed her time between attending carefully to my wants and walking along the dreary sands around Suez.

CHAPTER VI

VISIT TO MA'LULA

WE RELINQUISHED our intention of going to Mar Din, fortunately for ourselves, as otherwise we might have been eye-witnesses of the awful massacre at Urfu a few weeks later. But we judged that I might be the better for a little mountain air before returning home, so after going to Beyrout and spending a fortnight there, we sent for Joseph, drove in a little victoria to Damascus, and thence to two of the Syriac speaking villages in the Lebanon, 'Ain et Tineh and Ma'lula. The whole population of the former place came out to see us, as we were driving with difficulty after dark over what seemed more like a stony field than a road. They had kept firmly to the Christian religion from the early centuries of our era until a few years ago, when the men of the village desired to get rid of an unpopular sheikh, and saw no other way of doing it but that of going down to Damascus and taking the irrevocable step of inscribing themselves as Moslems. It served no purpose, however, for the sheikh had divined their intention, and had inscribed himself a Moslem a week earlier than they did. I can only wonder that the women did not make a protest.

These villages live on terms of peace and good will with their neighbours at Ma'lula, who, being the children of martyrs, have remained faithful to Christianity. The latter are in communion with the Church of Rome, though their one resident priest is married.

Ma'lula is one of the most picturesque towns we have ever seen. Situated in a narrow gorge, it clings to the face of a precipitous cliff, most of its houses being built in front of caves which form their back rooms. Its inhabitants are a fine stalwart race, chiefly engaged in baking, and of cleanly habits both in their persons and their dwellings. We might have stayed at the orthodox Convent of St. Thekla, which is built against the cliff opposite to the village, but we should thus have been shut out from seeking the life of the people; so we ordered the two little tents we had hired in Damascus to be pitched in an olive garden, and from the moment we arrived at 8.30 P.M. on Saturday, April 20th, till our departure on Tuesday morning, we were besieged, not to say mobbed, by a crowd of the villagers, who seemed to look on us in the light of a travelling show, and were never weary of watching us. The women helped to unpack and make our beds. The only chance of privacy we could get was by tying down the tent door, and even that exposed us to their reproaches when we ventured out again. Their language is a strange mixture of Syriac and Arabic, many words such as *sharagatha* ("tree"), *samakatha* ("fish"), being Arabic with Syriac terminations.

As the men brought various books for us to look at, I showed them the small edition of the Peshitta New Testament published by the American Bible Society. They were amazed when I told them that "New York" was on its title-page, and they looked rather serious when I said to them: "Your native tongue was the mother-tongue of our Saviour, it is being more and more studied by scholars in Europe and in America for the sake of the Gospels, and you are forgetting it, for what? For the sake of the tongue of the false prophet."

This is not, however, altogether their fault. Only loyalty to Christianity on the part of their heroic forefathers could have enabled them to resist the pressure of Arabic from without, but now when there is a school where grammatical Arabic is taught by a Christian priest, the acquiring of which enables the boys to get situations in Damascus, and is even a step to their emigrating to America, what chance of survival is there for the slip-shod corrupt Syriac?

The priest's wife constituted herself our cicerone. She showed us her husband's school, where girls and boys are taught together. The only reading books they have are devotional ones printed by the Jesuits in Beyrout, and this is of course infinitely better than a purely secular education. But it makes too little allowance for the playfulness and the versatility of childhood,—no pretty stories, no little verses, no simple explanations of natural objects, such as are found in our reading books at home, come in the way of these little ones. Whether this was due to poverty, or to the system pursued, I had no means of finding out without appearing to find fault.

Hannah, who seemed to have the same degree of social influence as is possessed by a rector's wife in an English country village, took us also on Sunday afternoon to a festive gathering, where everybody who was anybody was present. Climbing up the steepest narrowest streets, we found a crowd gathered in a grassy field, where young men were trying who could take the longest leaps, and pitch the heaviest stones; and a motley crowd was assembled round two rows of girls linked arm in arm who sang a very monotonous chant as they clapped their brown hands and hopped a step backward and a step forward by turns. They all wore flowing skirts and brilliantly embroidered jackets, with veils of dark spotted muslin or of white lace dependent from their graceful young heads. All displayed a profusion of coin-necklaces and other ornaments. An elderly, buxom, smiling woman had just begun to dance between the two rows of girls, when Mrs. Gibson created a diversion by taking the Frena out of its case, and trying to photograph them. The dance stopped, a crowd of restless unruly children intervened, and order was only restored after great efforts on the part of one of the men, by the dance recommencing. Mrs. Gibson again tried to photograph it, but again it ceased. Some of the girls squatted down on the grass to rest, and I sat beside them. They began asking me questions, and I was literally mobbed, a crowd of young eager faces pressing round me round in all directions. I told them what kind of fruits grow in England, when one girl put a handful of figs into my lap, and the others stuffed these with walnuts and insisted on my eating them. Then the crowd was suddenly increased by fresh additions, for the girls who had pressed round my sister in a similar way, had been dispersed by means of a stick. The next proposal was that we should join them in the dance, but we respectfully declined, and made our escape, returning to the priest's house through one of the narrow gorges and passing beneath a singular roof formed by a broken rock, from which in the olden days, people were hanged. We were followed by several men, who on entering, kissed the priest's hand and pressed it to their foreheads. They sat in a circle whilst we told them of our journeys to Sinai, and of the treasures we had found there. They said that the name of the dance was *dibki* in Arabic, *dabkatha* in Syriac. We also told them of a visit we had made to the North Cape to see the Midnight Sun. I fear they thought we were drawing largely on our imaginations.

After the priest, whose name was Jacob, had left for the evening service, we questioned Hannah about some of the Syriac words in use. The third person singular preterite of the verb "to be," is *wobi*; the demonstrative pronoun "this," is *hanna* and *hadda*; "there," is *door*; "son," is *ibri*; "daughter," *bracha*; "go away," *neppuq*; "come," *nekun zali*. Hannah had never heard the word *taliktha* for "a girl," nor *nuna* for "a fish."

I heard a little girl playing in the street called out to another "zali! zali!" This was curious, for the *i* of that word is not pronounced in Syria, but perhaps it was an Arabicism.

We were greatly interested in our visit to the Convent of Mar Thekla. It contained only three nuns, pleasant ruddy-faced women. The Abbess was distinguished by a fur lining to her robe, and took great pride in showing us the tomb of the first of women martyrs, and various rude little paintings commemorative of her life. She was greatly interested to learn that Thekla's is the first story of the series of saints' lives which over-lie the Gospels in the Syriac palimpsest which I had found at Sinai.

A short way from the Convent is a very narrow gorge betwixt stupendous cliffs, all honeycombed with tombs and caves. In one of the latter 1500 Christians found refuge during a massacre forty-two years ago, when many of the inhabitants of Ma'lula perished. The Roman Catholic Convent of Mar Serkiss is almost deserted. In fact it has only two monks, one of whom has found a home in the village, and the other was away.

Tuesday being the feast of Mar Serkiss, our friends were puzzled beyond measure as to why we could not stay to enjoy it. Fearful lest their hospitable importunity might detail us, we slipped away at half-past five in the morning, before many of them were up. On the high road we saw some caravans of camels laden with boxes of petroleum, setting off on the long journey from Damascus to Baghdad, and we were enabled to drive past a very large flock of sheep by the shepherd simply stepping off the road on to the hill-side, whither they all followed him. Heavy showers fell ere we reached Damascus, making us glad that we had not remained in our tents at Ma'lula, and we re-crossed the Lebanon to Beyrout amidst torrents of cold rain.

We reached home early in May, and I had no little difficulty in deciding in what form my transcription from the palimpsest text was to be published. It would have been comparatively easy to reprint the whole of the Gospels straight off, but I thought it would be more exact justice to the original transcribers and to myself to distinguish clearly between their work and mine, the latter having consisted to a great extent in the filling up of *lacunae*. I had also to consider my obligations towards the purchasers of the 1894 edition. So after much deliberating and consulting, I published a re-transcription of ninety-eight pages, in which the work done by Professor Bensly, Dr. Harris, and Mr. Burkitt appeared in black type, and that done by me in blue, and the pages were numbered and arranged so that they might be inter-leaved with those of the original edition. I also re-published my translation in a complete form.

There are several problems connected with the history of this manuscript which have hardly yet been noticed. The lines of the upper-writing, being in one column, extend from end to end of the present pages, and although they are bold and dis-tinct, each page contains many lines, the available space on it having been utilized to the utmost degree. This reveals the fact that vellum was scarce in the eighth century. The fourth century Gospel text is written in two columns. Whilst there is a space of considerably more than a centimetre between this and the inner edge of the leaf, it comes so near to the outer edge as sometimes almost to touch it. I cannot quite believe that its ancient scribe had so little idea of symmetry as to make the two margins so very unequal, for I have met with no instance amongst ancient MSS where the writing was not fairly straight upon the page. I therefore think that the leaves have been trimmed down so as to dock them slightly of their outer margins. Now why is the writing never cut into, as it was in the case of one of the Greek MS which John of Beth Mari utilized after he had finished with the Gospel one? Did he spare it from a feeling of reverence for its sacred character, or do we owe its preservation to a happy chance? In some instances, it has escaped by a rather close shave.

A second question is, at what period did vellum become scarce, and when was it again plentiful? There was no lack of it at Sinai in later centuries, if we may judge by the number of Greek, Arabic, and Syriac codices extant. Possibly the introduction of paper lessened the demand for it. The Gospel palimpsest has a secondary interest in being the very oldest of its species whose upper-writing bears a date.

CHAPTER VII

A LEAF OF THE HEBREW ECCLESIASTICUS

OF ALL THE JOURNEYS which my sister and I have made in the East, that in the spring of 1896 is the only one which was unwillingly undertaken; and yet it has been not the least fruitful in results. We had, in truth, resolved to spend the winter quietly at home, and devote ourselves to the proofs of the Palestinian Syriac texts which we had secured, when the news we received from Cairo seemed to indicate that there might be a chance of our finding something there. If we were to go to Egypt, we thought it would be well for us to see the manuscripts at Jerusalem also, the Mesopotamiam valley being then closed to all travellers, save those whose primary object, like that of our friends Dr. and Mrs. Rendel Harris, was to help the survivors of the late terrible massacres.

It is easy enough to get to Jerusalem; but on reaching Cairo, we found a not wholly unexpected obstacle in our way, quarantine, an experience which we have never yet undergone, and which our genial friend, Sir George Humphry, the distinguished surgeon, had pronounced to be, even in European lands, more dangerous than the cholera. Whether it be so or not, we were determined not to expose ourselves to it, especially on shore; and as we found that no steam-boat company would arrange for one of their vessels to stop at Jaffa, or even at Beyrout, so as to let the passengers get through the ordeal on board, we cut the matter short by determining to proceed to Jerusalem on dry land, or in other words, over the short desert to Gaza.

Leaving the train at Kantarah, we found our tents pitched on the Asiatic bank of the Suez Canal. Darkness brought on a vision of loveliness. Beneath the brilliant stars lay the broad strip of water which has made Africa an island, illuminated now by the red lights of the railway station, now by the weird beauty of the electric light. A blazing fire beside us showed a group of hardy Bedawîn sitting within a ring of spectre-like camels; then ever and anon we were summoned by the puff of a steam-engine to watch the stately progress of some large passenger-vessel, whose bows projected a magnificent flood of radiance into the darkness. Only a few feet of distance prevented us from shaking hands with some of our fellow countrymen who were journeying to and from the far ends of the earth, yet we retired to our quiet dinner table, and to our quiet beds, as if at home.

The road proved to be longer and much more difficult than we had anticipated. We thought in fact, that if Moses had led the children of Israel by this route instead of by Sinai, they would have had much more cause for grumbling. Progress over deep sand is difficult, even for camels, and walking was almost out of the question, except at the rare times when we came to a dried-up salt marsh. Water is occasionally met with, but it is so bad that our camels only sniffed, and refused to drink. Strangely enough, there is more vegetation in the form of little shrubs on these sand-hills than in the wadys of the peninsula, and the eye sometimes feasts on a bright patch of red poppies and large daisies growing on a sand-bank. We were in no danger of straying, for though the beaten path was generally covered up, the telegraph poles were always in sight.

We spent Sunday at the so-called river of Egypt, near the very rude fortified town of El Arish. The "river" is dried up, excepting for a few days in winter, its bed is so broad that it is difficult to tell where it begins or ends. We encamped near some groves of palm trees on its bank, and felt very much as if we were in one of the corners of the world. The following night we camped close to two upright stones which mark the frontier, and neither there nor at El Arish were we asked for the "teshkeri" or permit, which we had got with no little trouble at Cairo.

Gaza is a large town, picturesquely situated amongst groves of olives and oranges. After entering it we had to ride through a Moslem cemetery, where one of the festivals which celebrate the end of Ramadan was being held. Amongst the white grave-stones were a number of wooden swings and merry-go rounds laden with children, whose screams of delight filled the air. Some of the older boys ran after us and began to throw stones. I saw one bad-looking fellow put his hand under his coat as if to draw a pistol; I thought it best to laugh at him as if I took it for fun, but my sister's camel-driver was struck by a stone. We were afraid that the whole crowd would rush after us if anything excited them; and so were glad to find our tents pitched in a garden protected by a hedge of prickly cactus and by the British flag. We had to relinquish our intention of visiting the mosque, lest we should get into trouble, and Joseph procured two Turkish cavalry soldiers from the Governor to mount guard over our tents. Our impressions of the journey were embodied in the following lines:

From Egypt's fields of glowing green
    To Gaza's gardens gay,
Deep barren sand for ever drifts
    Athwart the traveller's way.

Six days beneath a blazing sun
    We press the yielding sod;
Where twice beside His mother rode
    The great Incarnate God.

His footsteps mark the line for ours
    On all our homeward way.
And still we pluck some fragrant flowers
    From spots where Jesus lay.

For since as man He conquered death,
    And chased its lurid gloom,
Our earth, that gave Him scanty breath,
    Hath glints of Eden's bloom.

One of the soldiers who had watched over us at Gaza accompanied us onwards to Jerusalem. His name was Mohammed, and as he was a very pleasant fellow, we asked him about his pay. He gets fifty francs (£2) a month, out of which he has to feed both himself and his horse, and pay for his uniform. He has also to provide his own horse. His pay would be spent in five days were it not that the peasants feed him. He just asks them for a chicken, and for the best barley, and a little tobacco, and sometimes for a little money. He is employed chiefly in collecting taxes. When a man does not pay his taxes within a reasonable time he gets the kourbash.

Our little luncheon tent was pitched at mid-day beside a village called Barbari, whose houses were built of mud and roofed with turf, reminding us of the fate of the wicked as described in the 129th Psalm. "Let them be as the grass upon the housetops, which withereth afore it groweth up. Wherewith the reaper filleth not his hand, nor he that binded sheaves his bosom."

Mohammed's horse feasted on the growing barley whilst we rested. We had some difficulty in ascertaining from the villagers which of the green hills around was Tell-el-Hesy, the site of Lachish, and of Dr. Frederick Bliss' excavations. A third of it has been cut away in the process of uncovering the remains of seven cities, each one super-imposed upon its defunct predecessor. Here Dr. Bliss found the famous tablet letter in the cuneiform character written by someone in Egypt in answer to one of the many similar tablet letters from governors of Canaanite cities which were found at Tell-el-Amarna, in Egypt.

We camped that night in a ploughed field, and supposed ourselves to be near the spot occupied by the army of Sennarcherib. It is curious to compare the story told by the Egyptian priests to Herodotus*, that the quivers and bow-strings of the Assyrians were eaten away by field mice, with the recent example we have had of plague infection being carried about by similar little animals—rats—in Bombay, and how Hezekiah himself nearly died of a disease which bore a remarkable re-semblance to that dreaded scourge (Isaiah xxxviii, 21).

We have a reference to this in the newly-recovered text of Ecclesiasticus,† not on the leaf which we were so soon to find, but on one of those which Professor Sayce was perhaps then carrying to Oxford— "And he smote the camp of the Assyrians, and discomfited them with the plague" (Ecclus. xlviii, 21).

We retained our camels between Gaza and Jerusalem, as the men assured us they could do the journey easily, and we should otherwise have had to wait a few days to procure horses in a very inhospitable town. But we were destined on that comparatively short road to meet with more mishaps than had ever fallen to our lot in the desert.

Our encampment on the night of March 18th was on the border-land between the life of the nomad and the settler. Some of the Bedawîn have taken to agricultural life, being encouraged to do so by the Government. They harness their camels to prim-itive ploughs, and build rough stone huts for their cattle, whilst they themselves continue to live in black tents. There is certainly more cultivation carried on throughout the whole of Judaea than there was when we visited in 1869. This must be a result of better

* Herodotus ii, 141. See on this subject Dr. Sinker's "Hezekiah and His Age," p. 142.
† See Messrs. Neubauer and Cowley's edition, p. 39.

protection to life and property, due probably to these regions coming so much under the observation of European residents and travellers. We may therefore conclude that British Consulates and Vice-Consulates in the interior of Turkey are not useless luxuries, and that a few more of them might have checked the Armenian massacres.

From Beit Jibrîn we sent on our tents in the direction of Beit Nettif, with orders to the sheikh to pass that village, and camp on the road to Jerusalem an hour before sunset, but on no account to go further than Allar-el-Foqa. We ourselves spent the day exploring various caves in the hill-sides, and if none of these have been certainly identified with the cave of Adullam, we thought it highly probable that they were once well known to the shepherd-poet of Israel. The sky was overhung with clouds, and sunset was approaching when we descended into the valley of Elah, memorable as the scene of David's encounter with Goliath. Every man we met was asked either by Mohammed or by Joseph if he had seen our tents, and the answer invariable was that they had gone further on, and that there were none pitched near the village. So we skirted the foot of the lofty green hill which bears Beit Nettif near its summit, and just as the moon rose we turned into the dry stony bed of a torrent forming the only path through a narrow valley. Mohammed dismounted, with the remark that he had once lamed a horse here, and we dismounted too, sitting down every now and then to discuss some biscuits. Worst of all, none of us knew the way, and a laden caravan which passed us, bound for Bethlehem, could give us no information. At last we descried a light and went towards it, but it was on the other side of the valley, and the repeated shouts of Joseph and the Bedawîn evoked no answer. We, however, turned into the valley where it was faintly gleaming, and as Mohammed bellowed out, *"Askâr, askâr, wa hanoum sittât!* ("A soldier, a soldier, and ladies of quality!") we saw a human figure moving amongst the rocks and coming towards us with a lantern.

It was a shepherd, who said that we were close to Allar-es-Sufla, and that he would guide us to Allar-el-Foqa. But he had been there all day, he said, and had seen no tents; also heavy rain had fallen, and the ground was wet. So we picked our way on foot between two walls on what might have been intended for a road, but was now a succession of mud pools interspersed with rocks. Over some of these Joseph tried to carry me, with the result that we both nearly fell. We tried the other side of one of the walls, but found only the wet heavy sticky clay of some olive gardens. It was nearly ten o'clock when we reached the mountain village of Allar-el-Foqa. Its dwellings, built of rough stones, were too dirty to receive us, so our only resource was to pitch our little square luncheon tent as a shelter against the wind, and spread the quilts from our camel-saddles within it on the wet ground. The Bedawîn lighted a great fire of brushwood before the open side of it, and we sat with them in a circle round it drying our mud-bespattered skirts. We could not but admire the intense good nature of these men who had been walking all day from half-past six in the morning, with a two hours' interval at noon. Yet the first care of one and all of them was for us. They roasted some coffee in a shovel, pounded it in a wooden mortar, and boiled it in a little tin pot. Mohammed brought several armfuls of tree-roots, which he had no doubt requisitioned, and cast them on the blazing pile. Everything he received from the villagers he shared with the Bedawîn, and they were evidently in no awe of him, though showing respect to his rather coarse uniform. Joseph bought some eggs and milk; these, switched up together, formed our evening meal, and then we tied down the door of the tent and tried in vain to sleep. The fire had attracted a number of insects, the coffee had been very strong, the damp penetrated through our quilts, our skirts were not half dry, and the wind was very cold. Joseph overheard one of us complaining to the other, and shoved in his own great-coat as an additional wrap. Our morning ablutions had to be performed in a biscuit tin, as no basin existed in the village; and no more coffee was to be had, so we were content with a little milk and a bit of almost uneatable bread before we started off with daylight towards Bittir.

After a wearisome ride over the mountains we descended to the village by a dangerously steep path, and found that for several miles our road ran along the rocky bed of a stream, often through the water. As wet stones are never safe for camels, and as we were very tired, we decided to sit for five hours under the olive trees, and take the afternoon train to Jerusalem. A party of Gaze's occupied the saloon carriage by which we travelled. They must have been alarmed by our dishevelled appearance until we explained about the loss of our tents. These were found, as we had hoped, pitched outside the Jaffa gate, close to the Upper Pool of Gihon. Our cook and waiter said they had been in despair at our non-arrival. A good dinner had been ready for us near Beit Nettif whilst we wandered in the dark over the almost trackless hills, and all concurred in putting the blame on a Bedawy who had been deputed to watch for us, and who didn't.

We remained quite happily in our tents for three days, walking over the little mountains which are round the city, and exchanging calls with friends. On the evening of Monday, March 23rd, the sky was overcast as we retired to rest, and we had hardly settled into our beds when a violent storm began. The rain, driven by a furious westerly wind, beat upon us in torrents, and penetrated partly through the roof, partly through the canvas wall of the tent, drenching my sister's bed. We rose several times, lit a candle, and fortified ourselves with some biscuits, besides placing all our available portmanteaus close to the windward side, so as to keep the canvas wall down by their weight. Owing to this precaution the tent did not collapse, but its floor had become a pond, on whose surface our boots and shoes were swimming leisurely about. The trench which had been dug outside was useless, for the water, collected on the grassy slope above, was flowing beneath our beds in an ever growing stream.

We packed all our superfluous clothes away, but flight could not be accomplished in the dark, and so we had to comfort each other as best we could till the first streak of daylight appeared. Such was the force of the wind and rain that our repeated shouts were unheard by the occupants of the kitchen tent, and these were made aware of our desires by the Turkish soldiers who had mounted guard over us, and who must have been very miserable themselves. By dint of shouting we made them understand that they must get a cab for us and take us to the Grand New Hotel, just within the Jaffa gate. A German cab-driver, roused from his slumbers, harnessed his horse, and took us off with several of our belongings; and very curious objects we were when we found refuge under the wing of M. Gélat, to the no small amusement of his other visitors. We escaped for a wonder without any immediate bad effect, but the discomfort we had endured probably laid the seeds of the complaint which sent me to bed for three months after our return home.

In the Grand New Hotel we stayed for four weeks amidst almost incessant heavy rain, continuing, with a few welcome breaks, until the middle of April. We employed our time photographing manuscripts both in the library of the Greek Monastery attached to the Church of the Holy Sepulchre and in the small Syrian Convent, whose church is said to occupy the site of the house of Mary the mother of Mark. We received a cordial welcome from the Greek Patriarch and from the Syrian Bishop, both of whom have lately passed into another world. In neither place, however, did we see anything half so valuable as the manuscripts at Sinai, and we could only work at very irregular intervals, owing to the time of the Greek Librarian being so much taken up with the Easter ceremonies.

We had thus abundant leisure for exploring Jerusalem, and noting the changes that have come over it since our visit to it more than twenty years ago. A new quarter has sprung up outside outside the walls to the north; it consists chiefly of European villa-like houses. The city has indeed travelled northwards in the course of the ages, for Dr. Frederick Bliss's excavations of the ancient city prove that this extended outside the present mediæval wall as far to the south as the modern suburb does to the north. It would be beyond the purpose of this book to speak of these excavations, of the fountain gate of Nehemiah, and of the stairs which led up to the city of David. These things, are they not all written in the books of the Chronicles of the Palestine Exploration Fund?

Nor must I linger to tell of the communion service which is held annually on the Thursday night of Passion Week in the little English church on Mount Zion, nor of how we walked through the city, along the Via Dolorosa, after dark, and sung a few hymns at Gethsemane, and then tried to realise on the "green hill," both on Friday afternoon and on Sunday morning, the awful scene of the Crucifixion, and that of the Resurrection.

In Jerusalem discussion waxed hot over the claims of the Green Hill and of the rival Church of the Sepulchre to be the site of Calvary. It is true that the claim of the Green Hill rests chiefly upon sentiment, the only fact it has in its favour being the undeniable resemblance of its shape to that of a skull. But the claim of the Sepulchre Church rests chiefly upon the "Invention of the Cross" by the Empress Helena, and our faith in this is greatly weakened when we know that she threw gold pieces to the workmen whom she employed in her researches. Tradition must count for little in this, seeing that no one of Jewish birth was allowed to enter the city for a century after its destruction; and one fatal objection to the Church of the Sepulchre, even if it should be proved to be outside the course of the second wall, is its low situation. If it be agreed that the place of the Crucifixion must have been in a conspicuous spot, visible from the greater part of the city, there is little choice left between the Green Hill, or "Gordon's Calvary," as it has been rather inaptly called, and the north-west corner now within the walls, where the Russian

Hospice is situated. The Church of the Sepulchre has been so much desecrated by squabbles, and by actual bloody fights between so-called Christians, that we would fain wish that the exact site may never be ascertained until our Saviour's prayer for His people's unity be fulfilled.

For the second time we witnessed the supposed descent of the Holy Fire on the Saturday of Passion Week. There were more Turkish soldiers and European spectators in the building than of yore, and fewer pilgrims, for the Armenians were expressly excluded. A free fight had taken place in 1895 owing to a misunderstanding between them and the Greeks; the head of our poor old friend, the Syriac Bishop, had been broken, the Armenian Patriarch had his beard completely plucked out, and a Turkish soldier was killed. Some of the pilgrims, whilst they waited for the appearance of the fire, formed a pyramid of their own bodies by standing on each other's shoulders in three tiers, and sang weird ditties, one of which Mrs. Gibson noted down, and we translated thus:

> Your feast, O ye Jews!
> The apes they would choose.
> Our feast is the feast of the Christ!
> The Christ He hath sought us,
> With His blood He hath bought us.
>> Right merry are we
>> When doleful ye be,
>>> O Jews!

This travesty of the Christian spirit may well be compared with our Lord's lament as recorded in Matthew xxiii, 37. Perhaps the antics of these people, like those of the dervishes, are a remnant of Baal-worship.

The idiosyncrasies of sincere believers have a free field for their display in the Holy City. One of these was related to us by Father Justin, the courteous Librarian of the Greek Patriarchate.

A lady from Chios was extremely desirous to see the site of Calvary as it is shown within the walls of the Church of the Holy Sepulchre. The monks who conducted her there were not surprised to see her fall on her knees, but they were unprepared for the fervent prayer which she offered: "O Lord Jesus! O Christ! why did you come to this stony place? Why did you not come to Chios? We have orange trees and lemon trees, and we have fine springs of water. Why did you not come to us? We would not have crucified you!"

We left Jerusalem on April 17th. Whilst there we had bought one large Hebrew MS of the Pentateuch, and we got a bundle of fragments from a dealer in the plain of Sharon. There was a similar bundle bought in Cairo, packed away in Mrs. Gibson's trunk, which she had sent on to Beyrout in the expectation that we should travel thither by land. This had now become impracticable on account of the rain, so we sent for the trunk from the Beyrout Custom House. It had never been really in the country, so the officials had no right to charge duty on any of its contents, but they would not let it go without the key. There is an obvious objection to having luggage over-hauled in the owner's absence, so we had to invoke the good offices of the Consul-General, Mr. Drummond-Hall, and it was accordingly sent by him to the care of the Vice-Consul at Jaffa. He in his turn raised difficulties. In the first place, being a Jew, he would not sign the order for its delivery to us on Saturday; and secondly, who was to guarantee to him that Mrs. Gibson was its actual owner, and not a person masquerading under her name? It was rather strange that he had on the previous day given us our letters without any questions. He was brought to reason by the production of our Foreign Office letter which had been granted to us the previous year, on the occasion of our proposed trip to Mar Din; but our troubles were not yet at an end, for the Custom House officials at Beyrout had sent a message to those at Jaffa to be very particular about that box, and they accordingly over-hauled and rumpled up everything that was in it, placing a heavy pair of boots on the top of a broché silk evening dress, and treating fancy creations of French millinery art as if they were like their own ragged uniforms. The bundle of Hebrew fragments passed of course under their scrutiny, and might possibly have been impounded had not Joseph come to its rescue. He took advantage of the law that exempts both the Bible and the Coran from the confiscation that is now extended to almost all other books. "Do you not see that these are Hebrew?" he exclaimed, "and the ladies say their prayers in Hebrew. Do you want to prevent them saying their prayers?"

This expostulation sufficed equally for the second bundle of fragments which we had bought only a few days previously. In fact, the officials were rather non-plussed at having found only some wearing apparel and some dirty scraps of vellum in a box which they had been told to examine particularly, so they let us off very easily when we finally departed on Tuesday. But we were grieved to see how roughly some grey-headed old men, intending emigrants, were treated, knocked about anyhow when they happened to be standing in anyone's way; and, worst of all how women were roughly torn away from their husbands on the gangway of our steamer, and forced to go back in the little boat, though frantic with grief at the prospect of half the round world lying between them and the fathers of their children. True, they had all been trying to emigrate without a Government permit, but they were doing this only when they had been subjected to delays which meant a practical refusal, and what good could result from bullying women when the men had escaped? We saw only a fringe of that detestable system of oppression which has converted so many fair regions of the earth into a wilderness, and which was, even at that moment, drenching the churches and valleys of Armenia with blood.

We reached home on May 3rd, and set about the work of examining out treasures and developing photographs. I had

arranged our fragments of the previous year, so I left our acqui-
sitions this time entirely in my sister's hands. She identified all
those amongst them which formed part of the Canonical Books
of the Old Testament, and as we thought that the rest were
probably either portions of the Talmud or of private Jewish
documents, we resolved on asking our friend Dr. Solomon
Schechter, Reader in Talmudic to the University, to examine
them.

Accordingly, on May 13th, I met him by chance on King's
Parade, and told him that we had a number of things at home
which awaited his inspection. He must have gone to our house
immediately, for I returned after doing a little shopping and
found him in the dining-room with our two bundles of fragments on the table. He held up a large vellum leaf saying, "This
is part of the Jewish Talmud★ which is very rare; may I take it
away?" "Certainly," I replied. Then he held up a dirty scrap of
paper. "This, too, is very interesting; may I take it away and
identify it?" "Certainly." "May I publish it?" I replied, "Mrs.
Gibson and I will be only too happy if you find that it is worth
publishing."

Dr. Schechter departed, and an hour afterwards we received
a telegram†: "Fragment is very important; come to me this afternoon." Again there came a letter as we were sitting down to
lunch. Here it is:

"UNIVERSITY LIBRARY, CAMBRIDGE,
"13/5/96.

Dear Mrs. LEWIS,—I think we have reason to congratulate ourselves. For
the fragment I took with me represents a piece of the *original Hebrew of
Ecclesiasticus*. It is the first time that such a thing was discovered. Please do

★ This has been since published by Dr. Schechter in the *Jewish Quarterly Review*
for October, 1896, p. 117.
† "Handed in at the Cherryhinton Road office at 1.26 p.m.; received here at
1.33 p.m." It was therefore despatched after the letter.

not speak yet about the matter till to-morrow. I will come to you to-morrow about 11 p.m. (*sic*) and talk over the matter with you, and how to make it known.—In haste and great excitement, yours sincerely, S. SCHECHTER."

We learnt afterwards that Dr. Schechter had confided the news of his discovery to the first people he met in the Library: Dr. Streane, Mr. Magnusson, Mr. Rogers, and others.

We went to his house in the afternoon, and at his request I wrote that same evening to both the *Athenæm* and the *Academy*, giving the dimensions of our leaf, the number of lines in its two columns of writing, etc. More than five weeks later, on June 27th, a notice appeared in the *Athenæm* to the effect that two of the learned Librarians of the Bodleian at Oxford had found nine more leaves of the same Hebrew text of Ecclesiasticus, which further examination has shown to belong to the same manu-script. Although this occurred in June, the fragments were brought to England by Professor Sayce almost simultaneously with ours, and it is natural for us to think that my letter of May 13th, published on May 16th, was of some assistance in guiding Messrs. Neubauer and Cowley to this important result. Yet it was bound to come sooner or later, for the Oxford leaves were in much better condition and more legible than ours, and I have been told that the first words which attracted attention were those of the characteristic passage: "Let us praise famous men, and the fathers that begat us."

Dr. Schechter published our fragment in the July number of the *Expositor*, then Dr. Neubauer and Mr. Cowley brought out the text of the whole ten leaves in the form of a book in the following January. Dr. Schechter, having observed the word "Fostat" on many of our Hebrew fragments, determined to investigate the source from which they all came, and for that purpose he repaired to Cairo at the close of the year 1896.

I ought perhaps to explain that our English version of

Ecclesiasticus, even the Revised one, has been made from Greek and Syriac translations; the former being by the grandson of the author, Jesus Ben Sira, about 132 B.C. The book itself does not contain an actual date, but the prologue to the Greek version states that it was made in Egypt in the thirty-eighth year of Euergetes, the King, and this pre-supposes that Ben Sira, grandfather of the translator, wrote the original text about 200 B.C.

Professor D. S. Margoliouth, of Oxford, had already made the advantages which would accrue from the reconstruction of the Hebrew of Ecclesiasticus the subject of his very brilliant inaugural lecture. I dare not, in the following questions, substitute the word "finding" for "reconstruction" or "restoration," but I leave it to the reader to do so mentally.

"Now the vocabulary which result from the restoration of Ben Sira, will be remarkable both in quantity and quality." p. 18.

"The reconstruction of the verses of Ben Sira, whether accomplished by me or by some abler Hebraist, will give us for Hebrew what has hitherto been wanting, a book of a certain date to serve as a sort of foundation-stone for the history of the language. If by 200 B.C. the whole Rabbinical farrago with its terms and phrases, and idioms and particles was developed, and was the classical language of Jerusalem, and the medium for prayer and philosophical and religious instruction and speculation, then between Ben Sira and the books of the Old Testament there must lie in most cases the deep waters of the Captivity, the grave of the old Hebrew and the old Israel, and the work of the new Hebrew and the new Israel." p. 20.

St. Jerome in the fourth century speaks of possessing a Hebrew copy, and R. S'adyah Gaon of Baghdad had access to one in the beginning of the tenth century; but after that period all quotations of Ben Sira's text appear to be at second hand.

The discovery was important, not only for its bearing on the history of the Old Testament Canon, but for the possibilities it suggested of further discoveries in the future. My sister and I may be excused for not having recognized the value of the leaf which we are now proud to possess. The Apocrypha is almost unknown to Scottish children, it is never put into their hands, and we were therefore not familiar with its text as we are with that of the Bible. Moreover, who even amongst scholars three years ago set any store whatever by Hebrew paper? Dr. Schechter, on the other hand, knows Hebrew as his native tongue, and had given special attention to Ecclesiasticus, having published a collection of the quotations from it that are found in the works of the Rabbis. He was therefore eminently fitted to be the pioneer in a series of discoveries of which we hope that we have seen only the beginning.

Another aspect of the matter affords us intense amusement and gratification. Sirach, the author of Ecclesiasticus, was a woman-hater. The names of Deborah, Ruth, and Judith do not occur in his lists of national heroes; and one of his aphorisms runs: "Better is the wickedness of a man than the goodness of a woman" (Ecclus. xlii, 14).

It seems therefore a just judgment upon him that the Hebrew text of his book, the text which he actually wrote, should have practically disappeared for fifteen centuries, and should have been brought under the eyes of a European scholar, I might say a scholar of his own nation, by two women.

CHAPTER VIII

A FOURTH VISIT
TO SINAI

ON THE VERY DAY which witnessed the discovery of the
Hebrew Ecclesiasticus I got a violent chill, whose immediate
cause—one which has cost many a valuable life—was that of
continuing to wear summer clothing after our return to
the damper climate of England. I had foolishly imagined that the
change would not be so great owing to the heavy rains we had
witnessed while in Jerusalem; and I paid for my temerity by an
attack of rheumatism and fever, which all but paralyzed me at
first, and sent me to bed for three months. One of my con-
solations was the dismal joke that I had been poisoned by
inhaling the microbe of Ecclesiasticus, a creature that may have
come into existence in the ninth century, and fattened on the
very dirty paper whereon Ecclus. xxxix, 15–xl, 8 was written.
Mrs. Gibson forsook every other occupation to nurse me with
devoted care, as one of our friends expressed it, "the sun seemed
to rise only for you." She managed to develop the greater part
of 800 photographs entirely alone; for they were finished when
she took me to Felixstowe in August. I had a relapse whilst there,
but after returning home in October I began to regain strength,
though the use of my limbs came back only with a ceaseless
struggle.

Mrs. Gibson was therefore not a little anxious when I

159

proposed a fourth trip to Sinai. I had the feeling that my aches would all be coaxed away if I could once get my feet on the warm sand and in June, when I was most rigid and immoveable, I had astonished her by asking if she was willing to go with me again, to make sure that we had got the text of the Palestinian Syriac Lectionaries of the Gospels quite correct. She would hardly have consented to this, however, even amidst the December cold, if I had not got encouragement from Dr. Donald MacAlister, who said the very best thing I could do was to go to a warmer country, and that I might as well try Cairo in the first instance; and if after a few weeks there I should feel equal to going further, I might try Sinai also.

Dr. Schechter wished us to accompany him to Egypt in December when the Michaelmas term ended, but this was not convenient for us, so we did not start until January 9th. Our movements were greatly stimulated, and my sister's objections over-weighted, by the news of Dr. Schechter's having obtained access to the Genizah synagogue, and having dived into a great hold filled with Hebrew fragments, both on paper and vellum, the accumulation of ages, from which both the nine Oxford leaves of Ecclesiasticus and our one leaf had evidently come, filtering to their present owners through the hands of thieves and more or less honest dealers.

I stood the journey much better than we had anticipated, and shortly after our arrival in Cairo we were taken by Dr. Schechter to see the Genizah. It is a very plain synagogue in one of the most densely populated quarters of old Cairo. A very broad gallery runs round three sides of it, and above one of these there is a door high up in the whitewashed wall, to which the roughest of rude ladders gave access. As its rungs were very wide apart, I dared not attempt to mount it; but the servant of the synagogue did so, and as he jumped down on the other side we could hear the crinkling of vellum leaves under his feet. Mrs. Gibson then mounted and peeped in, so did Miss de Witt, a Girton student whom Dr. Schechter had invited to accompany us. This loft has been likened by Dr. Schechter to a tomb of books. When a manuscript had become useless, the synagogue authorities would neither take on themselves the responsibility of destroying nor of selling a holy thing, so they just tossed it in there. The white-wash of the walls tumbled on it in the course of centuries, dust from the streets, not too pure, and sand from the desert blew in, a tap of water was turned on, whence it were perhaps better not to enquire, and the fragments all stuck together and got mixed in a way that is simply indescribable. The MSS at Sinai may have been exposed to rough usage, but they were at least protected by being packed up in boxes and baskets, and the most neglected of them never got torn up, nor was it ever exposed to being embedded in a heterogeneous mass of confusion such as filled the loft of the Genizah. One of the many regrets of my life is that on the occasion of our visit to it we left the little Frena in the hotel, and I am therefore unable to present my readers with a picture of its exterior.

The whole mass of ragged, jumbled, dirty stuff was presented to Dr. Schechter by the Grand Rabbi of Egypt. He had it packed into huge sacks, and as he could not be present in the gallery of the synagogue whilst this was done, still less could he personally conduct the sacks to the premises of a forwarding agent, some light-fingered gentry took the opportunity of having a last grab at the fragments. These were eventually sold in the Cairo shops, and a considerable quantity came into the possession of Mrs. Gibson and myself, with Dr. Schechter's full approbation. We bought a leather portmanteau to pack them into, and as there is no particular satisfaction in importing dirt, I sat down to the work of cleaning them in the bedroom of our hotel. This I did with great eagerness, for every scrap that I detached from its neighbours might possibly have been concealing another leaf of the Hebrew Ecclesiasticus, but in this I was disappointed. They were so wet that I had to spread them out on trunks and tables in the sunlight to dry, removing a quantity of sticky treacle-like stuff with bits of paper which I afterwards destroyed. This occupation was agreeably varied by an interesting tea party to which Dr. Schechter invited us along with Dean Butcher and his wife, in the Hotel Metropole, to meet the Grand Rabbi. He is a handsome young man who speaks no English, but many other languages. Mrs. Butcher and we exchanged a few ideas with him in Arabic and in Italian, but his conversation was chiefly with Dr. Schechter in Hebrew.

We took the portmanteau home with our personal luggage, and after removing from its contents all portions of the Canonical books of the Old Testament, we confided the rest to Dr. Schechter's care. He found that the larger part of this is interesting, simply on account of its antiquity. Three leaves show some faint Palestinian Syriac writing beneath Talmudic Hebrew, but none of them belong to the same MS as those published by Mr. Gwilliam in *Anecdota Oxoniensia*, Vol. I, Part V. One private document is dated A.D. 1038 and another A.D. 1149.

These last are of some scientific value on account of the composition of the paper. Portions of them have been subjected to a microscopic examination, and to a chemical analysis by Dr. Marshall Ward and Miss Dawson, and it is proved beyond doubt that they are made of flax that has never passed through the intermediate stage of rags.

Dr. Schechter found a home for his enormous spoil in some of the new rooms of the University Library at Cambridge, and he has had to face the gigantic task of cleaning, arranging, and identifying these. He has been rewarded for his toil by the discovery of some letters of Maimonides, written in Hebrew characters, though in Arabic; of some fragments of Aquila's Greek version of the Old Testament, the first of which was found by Mr. Burkitt; of many documents illustrative of Jewish history in the middle ages; and above all by more leaves of the Hebrew text of Ecclesiasticus, which he announced in the *Times* of July

1st and August 3rd, and which we confidently expect to see edited by him in the present year of grace.

I regained my strength when in Cairo to such a degree as to justify our making arrangements for another journey to Sinai. This was partly due to the warmer air, and partly to the attentions of a clever German *masseuse*, who restored to me the power of going up and down stairs in my usual way. We found greatly to our delight that the Khedivale Steamboat Company were willing to make one of their fortnightly vessels stop at Tor on its way to Djeddah and Suakim for the moderate sum of £5 in addition to our passage-money and the carriage of our stores. Tor is distant only three days' journey from Sinai, so there was a considerable saving to be effected in the item of fatigue.

At Suez we found the Greek shopkeepers greatly excited over the news of the massacre in Canea. We also met our old dragoman, Hanna, who was preparing to travel to Sinai by way of Wady Ghurundel in the service of Monsignor del Solar, a Roman Catholic Archbishop from Monte Video. On February 9th we embarked on board the steam-ship *Rahmanieh*. She was crowded with deck passengers in the form of pilgrims to Mecca, although we learnt from the telegrams of both London and Egyptian newspapers that the Sultan had forbidden them to go on account of the plague at Karachi and Bombay, and the great fear that this would soon extend to Egypt. Many of them must have made a circuitous journey, for we observed some of a type quite new to us, whom we mistook for Chinese, but who were really Afghans. We were the only women in the first class, and we received great attention from the captain, the engineer, the steward, and all the officials of the vessel, who vied with each other in trying to make us comfortable. We sat down to dinner in the company of eight Turkish gentlemen, who were greatly interested in the object of our journey, and not a little curious to learn how we had made such friends with the monks on Mount Sinai. They did not in the least understand that there is a common bond between Christians even when they follow very divergent ways of life.

Mrs. Gibson got into an argument with one of them as to how the plague was disseminated. She averred that the germs of it were fostered by the uncleanly ways of Orientals, and he insisted that they were carried about by travelling Europeans.

We had the ladies' cabin all to ourselves, and were in great anxiety lest we should sleep too long and be carried past Tor. We rose accordingly at 4.30, when it was hardly day, and managed to rouse the steward and get a cup of coffee. We might as well have spared both ourselves and him this trouble, as the *Rahmanieh* lay off Tor for the whole day, weighing anchor only at sunset, the reason being that she did not want to arrive at her next port of call during the night, and to be kept for hours waiting to land her merchandise.

Tor is a small group of substantial white houses, with a few groves of palm trees, on the fringe of the sandy plain which stretches from the base of the granite mountain ranges of Serbal and Sinai. It had one resident Englishman, Mr. Elton, quarantine storekeeper in the Egyptian service, who strangely enough came from a village near Cambridge. He took us ashore in his boat at nine o'clock. On the little quay we were received by a crowd of Arabs, whose faces beamed with smiles when we replied to their many salutations. An aged monk and two young ones came running amongst them, and gave us a most hearty welcome. They conducted us to the monastery, a very plain building. Its reception-room was adorned with heterogeneous pictures, the storming of Tel-el-Kebir by our gallant Highlanders and the bombardment of Alexandria side by side with an engraving of the high Priest Aaron, and a facsimile of the impress of Mohammed's hand, which he himself once gave to the Convent.

The monks offered us a little loukoumi and Turkish coffee. They had evidently heard some reports about our habits, for the usual tiny glasses of date brandy were conspicuous by their absence. It is quite a mistake for any traveller to think that he or she is obliged to drink this. Turkish coffee has a fine aroma, and is much more refreshing than that made in the European way, but as it is not strained, you must take care to leave the dregs, else you will have *grounds* of complaint against it. And you do not get more than three sips at a time.

After talking for an hour, chiefly about Cretan politics, we walked to our tents under the palm trees. The fowls which Joseph had brought from Suez were liberated from their crates on to the sand, and three pairs of cocks instantly flew at each other. They were only tiny scraps of birds, all feathers and hardly any bodies, yet they ruffled up their small combs, opened wide their little beaks, flapped their puny wings, and breathed mortal defiance as valiantly as if they had been belted knights. This comic tragedy was frequently re-enacted after we were encamped in the Convent garden. Joseph or the gardener used to put a stop to it, but the combatants were more effectually separated by a great black turkey, who took to acting policeman, and walked up in a stately way whenever a row began.

Mr. Elton took tea with us, and told us of the straits to which the natives were sometimes driven for the want of a doctor. Five days previously an Arab carpenter split his finger with an adze, and as he happened to possess a bottle of phenic acid, probably stolen from the quarantine stores, he poured its contents on the wound, with the result that his arm swelled, and he was nearly out of his mind with pain. He came for advice to Mr. Elton, who could only suggest that the might steep the arm in warm water, and so try to draw some of the poison out of it. Another had cut the sole of his foot on a bit of broken glass while wading after lobsters. His friends had burnt it, and then he had not the sense to refrain from walking, and a dangerous inflammation had set in.

A strong sea-breeze shook the canvas of our tents that night.

Some of the spots close to the village are not considered healthy for camping on, owing to the nature of the ground, but we were glad to observe that travellers may embark and disembark here without necessarily coming into contact with the occupants of the quarantine station, which is at a considerable distance from the town.

We started next morning (Feb. 11th) at 7.45, and walked for an hour across the plain to the little village of El Wadi, nestling in palm trees, then sat down and awaited the coming of our camels for nearly an hour. Joseph at last appeared, and said that the members of the four tribes who formed our caravan had quarrelled over the money he had paid them. They had almost fought, and had tried to make him agree to take a somewhat longer road by way of Feirân, because the one by Wady Hebrân had been spoilt by the rain. We did not believe this, for we had been told by Mr. Elton that none had fallen since New Year's Day. We walked for an hour further to the village of El Kuram, then mounted and rode through a beautiful grove of palm trees, then over a barren plain dotted with sand hills and limestone shingles, the *débris* of many a flood. Soon we struck into what had the form of a road in the sand, the Bedawîn explaining that Abbas Pasha's road lay beneath it. As a strong cool wind was blowing from the sea, our luncheon tent was pitched with some difficulty, and we had actually to help by holding two of its cords during the process. We could not help thinking how great an addition to our comfort a little bit of canvas like this would have been in our three former journeys, when we frequently experienced a difficulty in finding sufficient shelter from the noon-day sun. It served the purpose likewise of a dining tent for us two whilst we camped in the Convent garden.

Starting again at half-past two, we walked and rode for three hours over an expanse of gravelly sand studded with bits of the pink Sinai granite. At 5.30 we found our tents pitched in a depression of the ground in face of the magnificent mountain range where it is pierced by the Wady Hebrân. I was very tired, but yet I was disappointed at our stopping so soon, having understood from Miss Buxton's book that her father's first encampment had been at the mouth of the wady.

After a very quiet warm night we started at 7.45 on February 12th, and walked along Abbas' sand-covered road to the foot of the mountains. At nine o'clock we mounted and entered the Wady Hebrân, where the road was completely obliterated by fallen boulders and stones. We picked our way above it till we reached a pretty stream, tumbling over the rocks and forming a succession of pools. Sometimes in a sunny place it gradually dwindled till it became a mere thread of water, to re-appear again in the shade. We dismounted, and clambered over rocks between craggy cliffs for an hour, passing sometimes amongst lovely little groups of palm trees, and then re-mounted as the valley opened out a little and Abbas' road re-appeared. We stopped at 11.30 and lunched beneath some palm trees whose stems had been scorched by Bedawîn fires. The wind was wonderfully cold.

We re-mounted at 2.15, and after passing another pretty grove of palm trees, we rode for two hours along a narrow stony wady hemmed in by rugged granite cliffs, and then began to ascend some shingly hills by a narrow winding path, where we thought it wise to dismount. For three hours and a half we trudged up and down these spurs of the mountains, always hoping to catch a sight of our tents, or at least to descry ground where it might have been possible to pitch them. Twice Joseph persuaded us to mount our camels, but I nearly fell off mine whilst it was going up hill. I had not yet recovered the power of bending my knees, so when my feet were jerked up I could do nothing to keep them down, and I had to shout for help to prevent myself falling over the animal's back. I was quite unable to spring either up or down, so Joseph had always to lift me both in mounting and dismounting.

We blamed the sheikh for our present trouble. He had lost nearly an hour before starting on the previous day, so that this day's journey was an hour longer than it ought to have been. Also when he had passed us at noon, and we had told him to go on for three-and-a-half hours further, he never gave us the least hint that the first spot suitable for camping would be at least five hours distant. Had we known that such a rugged way lay before us we should have spared ourselves the early walk, and by riding until half-past twelve, and re-mounting at two o'clock, we could have accomplished the journey by daylight. Three hours after sunset we espied the red light of camp fire, some miles beneath us in the Wady Solaf, and this encouraged us to persevere, thankful for the faint moonlight which helped us to crawl to our tents. Just before it became dark we espied a beautiful namûs (or pre-historic house), with a perfect door to it, on a little hill to our right. We had walked ten miles since mid-day.

Next morning (Feb. 13th) we started at 7.40 and went along the Wady Solaf, much beset by the children from a Bedawy encampment clamouring for backsheesh, passed the mouths of the Wady Kabrîn and Wady Itla', then mounted into the Nugb Hawa, and rested for lunch under a great stone which had served for a similar purpose on one of our previous journeys. We walked on till the peak of the Râs Sufsafah burst on our view, and then rode to the middle of the plain, where we dismounted and took photographs, reaching the Convent at 5.30 on Saturday afternoon.

CHAPTER IX

OUR FOURTH STAY AT THE CONVENT

WE RECEIVED a cordial welcome at the door from several monks, but they did not ask us to enter the Convent as it was near their time for shutting it up. Father Euthymios came into the garden to greet us as we were taking off our hats. He had been promoted to the office of Bursar, which he well deserved, for a more trustworthy active man cannot be found anywhere. He proposed that we should attend the early morning service, which was to begin at dawn. This I was utterly unable to do, especially as it was so bitterly cold, the snow on the summit of Sinai not being quite yet melted. We placed our little beds together and spread all our coverlets over them both; thus doubling our means of warmth. At 2 A.M. we were awakened by a chime of sweet-toned bells, which appeared to last for fifteen minutes, and was re-echoed from the cliffs in all directions. We knew that a service was being held in the little white garden church close to us, in whose crypt the bones of defunct brethren are exposed in their habitual robes after having been buried for a year. We never visited the ghastly place, for we were sleeping within a stone's throw of it, and we did not want the night-mare. And as we felt the snow-cold touch of the air on our faces, even within the tent, we were deeply thankful that no law, divine nor human, obliged us to get up and kneel on the stone floor of the church.

Euthymios came to call us while it was yet dark, but we missed the service, and took a walk, and my sister coaxed me into climbing Jebel Moneijah. It commands a splendid view of Wady Zeitun on the one side and of the Wady-esh-Sheikh on the other, also of the range beyond the Nugb Hawa. But it was dangerous work for me coming down over the loose shingle, with only an occasional red rock to hold on to. We resolved never again to go so far without a guide. Yet I was not long in discovering that the more I climbed the more I drove the rheumatic stiffness out of my limbs.

We could not help thinking that the children of Israel underwent a physical preparation, as well as a moral one, in the wilderness for their conquest of Palestine. The generation which had spend their childhood breathing the pure dry mountain air of Sinai, and leaping amongst its rocks, must have possessed characteristics very different from those of the poor cowed slaves who had been reared on the rich plains of Egypt.

The almond trees in the Convent garden were now a mass of white flowers. It was more than pretty to see our white hens walking along their branches in search of little tit-bits in the shape of buds. The old gaunt cypresses had been cut down, and fresh young ones had taken their place. Copious rain had indeed made this little oasis in the wilderness to blossom as the rose.

One great change had taken place within the Convent walls, the disappearance of the mosque. This had fallen down for want of repair, leaving only its tower standing. More of the buildings around it are threatening to collapse, and, as Father Polycarp remarked one day, the church is the only solid building in the monastery, which thus became to us as a type of the world without.

Two Italian gentlemen, the Cavaliere Emilio Silvestri and his secretary, had encamped in the garden before our arrival. They were accomplished photographers, and were intent on trying their skill on some of the MSS before proceeding to Petra. On

Monday morning we found it impossible either to enter the Convent or to get through the outer courtyard gate, on account of the departure of 100 Russian pilgrims. The Italian gentlemen and we tried to console ourselves and each other for the loss of time by going amongst these people and taking snap-shots of them with our Kodaks, to the great delight of those whose portraits we carried off. Some of the women came about our camp, and the gaudy lining of our luncheon tent made one of them, who spoke a little vulgar Greek, say "like a palace." Her ideal of magnificence was truly not a high one. We at length effected an exit, and were clambering over the rocks, when one messenger after another came to say that the Archbishop was ready to receive us. His Grace welcomed us with his usual affability, and we had a long conversation, chiefly about the desirability of having the palimpsest bound.

We then accompanied the Italians to the library, and the palimpsest was at once produced without our asking for it, lying in its box, and wrapped in Mrs Bensly's cover. It had evidently suffered nothing from recent treatment, and it was a source of great satisfaction to me that my application of the re-agent had nowhere left a permanent stain. This had been very variable in its effects, however, some of the words which had been coaxed up by it remaining clear and distinct, such as those of the final colophon on f. 139^v, whilst others, such as those on the page containing the Angels' Song in Luke (f. 138^r), had completely disappeared, but were ready to come up again, the surface of the vellum being there quite smooth and unscratched.

I spent a week in trying to get a few more words out of it, but my success was small, as it had been so well squeezed already. The little I did get was published in the *Expositor* for August, 1897.

Mrs. Gibson and I thenceforward devoted our energies to comparing the sheets of our forthcoming edition of the two Palestinian Syriac Lectionaries with the originals. The first of these had been a great favourite with Father Galaktéon, who called my attention to it in 1892, whilst I was engaged with the palimpsest. Only one visitor to the Convent had ever been able to read it, he said. He asked me to photograph a few pages, that I might exhibit them in Europe, and find out what they were. I did so a week later, and I was then seized with an irrepressible wish to read them for myself. This I managed by placing Dr. Euting's table of Semitic alphabets before the manuscript and my own eyes for an hour every morning. In six days by following this plan I was able to announce, to Galaktéon's delight, that it was a Lectionary which began with John i, 1 and finished with the story of Herodias in Mark vi.

Before this time there was only one specimen of a complete book in this language—the form of Aramaic spoken by our Lord—the Galilean tongue also, which betrayed St. Peter. This was the famous *Evangeliarium Hierosolymitanum* of the Vatican Library, dated A.D. 1030, discovered by the Maronite Stephen Evodius Assemani in 1750, described by Adler in 1789, and edited first by Count Miniscalchi-Erizzo in 1864, and afterwards by the late Dr. Paul de Lagarde, and published in 1891 amongst his posthumous works. It has been valued chiefly as being a translation from Greek MSS which are no longer extant, and thus constituting an independent witness to the genuine character of the Gospel narrative. It is identified with the mother tongue of our Lord through its close resemblance to the Aramaic of the Targums, and with the mother tongue of St. Peter from the fact stated by Dr. Gustav Dalman, and that the Jewish Rabbis who fled from Southern Palestine after the persecution under Hadrian took refuge in the villages of Galilee, and that thenceforward their erudition robed itself in a Galilean dress. Many fragments of Palestinian Syriac had been found and edited by Dr. Land, Dr. Rendel Harris, and others, but nothing further in the form of a complete book.

After I had developed my four specimen photographs in

172

Cambridge, Dr. Rendel Harris and others told me that the manuscript was nothing less than a second copy of the *Evangeliarium Hierosolymitanum*, which was thus dethroned from its unique position. I went to Sinai in 1893 prepared to make a complete collation of it with Dr. de Lagarde's text, and on the afternoon of our arrival Dr. Harris doubled my work by discovering another copy of the same amongst the batch of books which were brought out of the palimpsest. The editing of these two MSS has been the joint work of Mrs. Gibson and myself. It has proved a more troublesome task than we anticipated, and as the Cambridge University Press had not sufficient type for it and for the palimpsest Gospels at the same time, we confided it to the care of Messrs. Gilbert and Rivington.

We failed, both in 1895 and 1897, to obtain a sight of any of the little ragged fragments of Greek and Syriac MSS which Father Galaktéon asked Dr. Rendel Harris to catalogue in 1893, because on both occasions we enquired for them after the Archbishop had departed with the key of a certain cupboard in his keeping. If all the MSS which these represent had remained intact, they would form a collection second to few in the world. Dr. Harris kindly gave me his list for insertion in my Catalogue of Syriac MSS. The gem amongst them was the Greek leaf which he numbered 8, containing the double ending to St. Mark's Gospel, known hitherto only in Codex L.

Mrs. Gibson photographed the whole of a little eighth century Arabic MS which had been brought to her by the monks in 1892 amongst the first batch of Arabic MSS which she catalogued. After she had read enough of it to label it, it attracted the notice of Professor Bensly, who advised Mrs. Burkitt to copy portions of it. Some of these have been published by Dr. Merx in the *Zeitschrift für Assyriologie*, and the text of the whole MS will appear, edited by Mrs. Gibson, as No. VII of the *Studia Sinaitica*.

We have been less fortunate with the Codex of the Arabic Gospels which we photographed in 1892. Professor Caravacek, of Vienna, and Dr. Robertson Smith judged them to belong to the tenth century.

Whilst we were preparing for our second journey, Mrs. Gibson and I saw that we must arrange our work in such a manner as to make sure that we had a complete coy of this text, and of the text of the Codex of Arabic Epistles, since published as *Studia Sinaitica*, No. II. Our plan was to transcribe them both from the photographs at home, leaving blank spaces where these were illegible, owing to the intrusion of light on the negatives, dirt on the manuscript, fog in development, or other causes. It was perfectly impossible for us to do the whole of this work in time to take the copy with us, so Mrs. Gibson undertook to transcribe the text of the Epistles, and we confided that of the Gospels to a native Arab who happened to be in London at the time, paying him a shilling a page, or ten pounds for the whole work, and instructing him to leave blanks for what he could not read. As I was packing up the last leaves of his copy to put it in my box, I observed that a corner of one of the photographs was perfectly white from the effects of an intrusive sunbeam, and yet there was no blank to correspond to it on the written page. So I called the scribe to account for this, and asked him where he got these verses. He replied, with an air of self-complacency, "That is just what they ought to be. I filled up everything I could not read from the British and Foreign Bible Society's version, as it was edited by Dr. Van Dyck!"

We still made an effort to get the text of these Gospels by taking the photographs and comparing our scribes's copy with the manuscript wherever these were indistinct, also by re-photographing fifty defective pages, so as to have the means of checking unwarrantable interpolations. But another misfortune occurred. Whilst we were taking the film-rolls on which these had been imprinted out of our Eastman boxes, with the help of a red lamp in the sanctuary of our tent, a brilliant white light was flashed around. Ahmed, forgetful of our orders to have no light in the camp which would interfere with our changing films for at least an hour after dinner, had lit a magnesium light, partly to ascertain if any dogs or thieves might have been accidentally shut into the garden, and partly, I suspect, to gratify his Arab love of display. Fifty-four photographs, representing more than two hours' work, were ruined. I fear I was cross, but I think I had provocation. Ahmed was only made to comprehend the nature of the mischief he had done by being told that the ruined films had cost twenty shillings. We were too much disheartened to do anything further with these unlucky Arabic Gospels.

On February 16th we found the Convent door closed on our return from lunch, and it was nearly an hour before we could gain admittance. There is no bell, and a battering-ram could make no impression on the solid structure. It is always closed during church services and during meals, so we had to learn to time our entrances and exits with these important events; and our hour of waiting was passed in very pleasant conversation with the Cavaliere. The Archbishop honoured us with a visit at tea-time, and was greatly amused by our description of the battles in our poultry-yard, which were as much outside of his experience as they were of ours.

On Feb. 17th the Archbishop of Monterides in Uruguay arrived, with Hanna Abu Sa'ab. The Italians set to work very energetically with their cameras; they produced splendid groups of the monastic family, a dark room being placed at their disposal. The Convent underwent a photographic bombardment; no less than nine cameras and Kodaks were going at once, two belonging to Monsignor del Solar, five to the Italians, and two to ourselves. We had a most interesting tea-party in our little dining-tent. The story of the Israelites was discussed in racy Italian, and with a freedom which I would not have believed possible among Roman Catholics. All agreed that it was im-possible for anyone who has seen the Râs Sufsafah, with the great plain of Er-Rahah lying before it, to admit the claim of any other mountain to be the scene of the giving of the Law. Our visitors considered that the reason which induced the children of Israel to leave Egypt was that the feeling of nationality had come strongly upon them. This was a very natural view for Italians to take. Monsignor del Solar, being a Spanish-American, speculated on what would be done with this little strip of desert country, and with the Holy Land, if they had existed on the other side of the Atlantic. Roads would have been made and every possible facility would have been given for the passage of pilgrims and of travellers, instead of being all left to these stupid Bedawîn. There is another side to the picture however, for the whole country might possibly have been vulgarized.

His Grace was deeply interested in hearing all that we could tell him about the palimpsest, and as he shared my views about the risk to which it was being exposed for want of a binding, I asked him to speak again to the Greek Archbishop about it.

The Italians left for Petra next morning. Their departure was preceded by the usual stormy negotiations in the courtyard of the Convent between their dragoman and the quarrelsome Bedawîn of the Akabah region. Father Euthymios presided over the discussion for several hours, and plenty of bad language was flying about. I wished to seize the opportunity of studying this branch of Semitic science; but the loud voices dropped and the uplifted hands fell whenever I tried to make my way into the centre of the throng, so I was baffled in my laudable efforts. I could not help recollecting a similar scene in 1893, when a party of Latin priests were leaving. Father Nicodemus acted as umpire on that occasion, and Ahmed, who was deeply impressed, shrugged his shoulders, saying, "I shall never take a party to Petra; I will not expose myself to being called a dog like that man."

The party must have had an unpleasant journey, for it was cloudy and bitterly cold towards evening, and there was a high wind with some showers of hail the following night. This did not deter the Roman Catholic Archbishop from departing also on the path to Petra. We were glad to retire from the little tent with its open front and dine in our bedroom.

On the following Monday, Feb. 22nd, I had a great fight with our Eastman film-boxes. We had neglected the precaution of sending them to the establishment in Oxford Street to be regulated before our departure from home, and they had both been lying unused for six months. The consequence was that one of them refused to work at all, and the other got so loose after two photographs had been taken as to be quite useless. The wooden roller attached to the register would not keep firm, and was all the time working its own screw out. We were at our wits' end to know what we should do; we had seven hundred beautiful films, the material was lying in the Convent to employ them on, and they were all to be wasted because of the perverseness of these boxes. I turned the matter over in my dreams, and at last I came to a desperate resolution. I would put my thumb on the loose screw, and hold it in its place whilst I wound off the film. From the first moment that I did so the rebellious box worked like a clock; it nicked our exposures at the exact place, and we worked up all our films with it, re-filling it once every morning in the dark room which the Italian Cavaliere had first used.

Edwards' films did beautifully also in the backs of our camera, being thicker. They give finer photographs than the Eastman rolls do, but if they are not put in perfectly straight an accident sometimes occurs whilst closing the shutter, and the film gets light in it. These spoilt films were used to make what we called "concoctions." A bit of the Eastman roll film was taken an inch longer than an exposure ought to be; its ends were folded over one of the spoilt Edwards' films, and it was placed in one of the backs.

The picture was taken on it whilst the spoilt thick film kept it in its place. By this means we used up the ends of rolls which

had got damaged whilst we were fighting with the two recalcitrant boxes.

With the Italians went a playful little brown dog named Foxie,
which had frolicked its way into our affections. It came into the
tent whilst we were dressing, and gambolled at such a rate that
nothing could be done till it was put out. Most amusing and
pathetic were its attempts to make friends with a large furry
pariah dog, who had never in its life seen a fellow creature so full
of fun. These poor dogs shrink with terror from every human
being who passes them. The Bedawîn throw stones at them often
simply for amusement. They eke out a precarious existence too
often on carrion, and unless they attain a degree of respectability,
as our friend Dick did in 1893, by attaching themselves to some
caravan or encampment, they are literally nothing but skin and
bone. Imagine the astonishment then of a canine patriarch of the
desert when a little sleek, wiry black-eyed ball of a thing jumps
up at his ears and asks him to play, then takes the same liberty
with the men and women he so much dreads, getting in return
not kicks, but caresses.

A dog is greatly raised in the scale of being when it is associ-
ated with the higher personality of man; and this may help us to
understand how man himself is exalted by communion with the
nobler specimens of his own race, and how these in turn owe
their superiority to a more vivid appreciation of their relationship to the Creator, especially if they have learnt to know Him
as He has manifested Himself to us in the Man, Christ Jesus.

One of the two dogs which Joseph had allowed to remain in
the garden took to barking furiously at night, and as he quite
murdered our sleep and nothing would cure him, he had to be
banished to the outside desert. Another of our pets was a little
gazelle, sole survivor of a pair which the Bedawîn had once
presented to the monks. It would come very near, and even take
biscuits out of our hands, but no one could succeed in actually
touching it. After sunset it sometimes played at a game of leaps

by itself, bounding amongst the trees for several hundred yards with the swiftness of an arrow. Yet another was a little black hedgehog, which Joseph picked up one evening on the stony path which leads to the summit of Jebel Musa. He tied a string to its leg, and led it, or rather followed it about. We named it Hajy, and kept it about a fortnight, then the poor thing died of cold after refusing to take its food, on a windy night.

The Archbishop left on Feb. 24th with the customary salute of bells, gongs, and cannon. On the previous evening he explained to us his reasons for deciding not to have the palimpsest re-bound. The upper-writing comes quite close to the edge of the leaves on the inner side, and the cord which formerly held them together has made holes, round which the vellum is very crumbly. To sew these leaves together again would be impossible, and as for the plan of pasting on strips of paper, this would need to be done by a more skilful hand than any that is to be found in Cairo. I suggested that His Grace might take it to Paris and entrust it to the binder of the *Bibliothèque Nationale*. He replied, "Then I would have to stand over him, and watch him put in every leaf. In the meantime I must just trust to three things for its preservation—to its silken cover, to its box, and to the conscience of those who study it."

Our sheikh sometimes entertained us with a very primitive performance on a stringed instrument called a *rebaba*. This he did after dark, squatting under the olive trees, his picturesque white garments and swarthy limbs illuminated by the red light of a Chinese lantern, whilst our Arab servants and the Bedawy gardener listened with open-mouthed delight.

One morning we were both startled and delighted by the appearance of our old friend Mushaghghil. He was very effusive in his expressions of regard for us, but though dying of curiosity, we did not venture to transgress the laws of Moslem etiquette by asking about his two wives. The sheikh, however, was in-terrogated after his departure, and he summed up the situation in two words, "Divorced both!" Mrs. Gibson's prophecy had been very soon fulfilled.

Sometimes our walks extended up a little wady on the other side of the Râs Sufsafah, approached from another corner of the great plain. There the ruins of a convent nestle in a garden containing twenty flowering almond trees and a palm tree, over-shadowed by a lofty crag crowned by a ruin like an acropolis, and a cistern for rain-water. The monks called the place Kourkodillo.

Sometimes 'Amr the sheikh accompanied us in our evening rambles. He told us that before the canal was made, the Bedawîn used to cross the Red Sea with their camels on their way from Cairo, half-an-hour above the spot on the canal bank where travellers usually land in going from Suez to 'Ain Musa. The water came up sometimes their knees, sometimes to the saddles of their camels. It was higher in winter than in summer. The camel can swim, but he has to be forced to do so. How easily at such a spot could a strong east wind cause the water to go back, without any great interference with the laws of nature!

Mrs. Gibson and I find no difficulty in believing that Divine Providence has sometimes visibly intervened in the affairs of men, but that in every instance the utmost possible use has been made of natural forces already existing. My sister once made poor Father Galaktéon very angry by expressing some doubts as to the great boulder, which Father Euthymios showed us near the ruined Convent of Arba'în, being the genuine rock struck by Moses. She was persuaded that the real subject of the miracle recorded in Exodus must have been a living rock, for she had a theory that possibly Moses was directed to tap a store of water that had been laid up in the granite by winter rain and snow. Galaktéon became greatly excited. "You come from Scotland," he said. "Was Moses ever there? If he was not, how are you able to come and tell us what he did?" When his anger was appeased, he proposed to take us for a walk in the afternoon, and show us what he believed to be the real rock.

Another hypothesis of my sister's is that a variety of languages was gradually developed after the descendants of Noah had become scattered, and the various tribes had been separated from each other by rivers and mountains; and that they discovered the wide divergencies of speech only when they were brought together for the purpose of building the Tower of Babel. Hence arose the notion that God confounded the language of all the earth (Gen. xi, 9); but none the less did it happen according to the purpose of His will.

We cannot quite understand the force of one of the arguments which is sometimes adduced in support of the theory that Exodus and Deuteronomy could not have been written in the Sinai desert, I allude to the term "seawards" for westwards in Exod. xxvi, 22, 27; xxxvi, 27, 32; Deut. iii, 27. The expression seems quite a natural one to those who have entered the peninsula by way of Suez, and have spent the first days of their journey in skirting the shore of the Red Sea. Reason, report, and the map may alike tell them that there is a larger sea to the south and east, but for them "seawards" will always suggest the direction in which they themselves have actually seen the blue expanse, and in which it can be seen from the top of Sinai, viz. towards the west. The same expression might of course be used by a writer living in Palestine, but as it comes naturally in both places, it seems to us a very slender basis for the argument which has been built upon it.

CHAPTER X

HOMEWARDS

W<small>E LEFT THE</small> C<small>ONVENT</small> on March 16th, bidding adieu to our kind friends, with the more regret that the political outlook for their country was so gloomy.

On the eve of our departure we had what was an ideal dinner for the desert—soup, roast wild gazelle (not our little frolicsome pet), beans, and stewed apples. Joseph had provided royally for us on this trip, having constantly procured fresh milk and mutton from the Bedawîn, and having brought magnificent specimens of asparagus and other tinned vegetables from Cairo, not to speak of the turkeys and the quarrelsome cocks. It is curious to note a statement of our dragoman's that there was no spot at which we encamped in 1897 betwixt Sinai and Wady Ghurundel, where he could not have bought a sheep had he been so minded. Indeed, one night near Sarabit-el-Kadim, the owner of two animals came pestering us whilst we rested at our tent door with shouts of "*Samîn! Samîn!*" ("fat! fat!"). It was touching to see how the trustful creatures followed him about all unwitting of his nefarious designs on them. They are of the broad-tailed variety, and have very strong legs and hoofs, for they are inured to climbing. We were glad that these individual ones were not bought.

On March 17th we lunched in Wady Ratamah under a great fallen rock, which had given shelter to ourselves and to Hanna in 1892. It forms quite a roof of stone, and before it was a white flowering *ratam*-bush (or broom), amongst which the bees were humming. This is the juniper-tree, one of the species that gave shelter to the weary prophet Elijah (I Kings xix. 4).

We found a great deal more vegetation in Wady Bark and in the pass leading up to Sarabit-el-Kadim than we had ever seen there before. In the latter there were actually many sweet little daisies, and some cultivated plots sown with beans near the path which leads up to the temple.

The chief sheikh of two tribes, the Alizah and the Jebaliyah, accompanied us from Sinai for the sake of company. They rode along with us instead of attaching themselves to our baggage caravan. The former left us in the Wady Tayibah, with many protestations of friendship for Joseph; the latter was an aged man with bright eager eyes, and two remaining front teeth. They seemed to be on terms of perfect equality with their kinsmen who were in our service.

Leaving the Wady-el-Bark on March 18th, we encamped on a dreary, sandy upland, the sheikh explaining that he could not take us into the pretty little wady where we encamped with Hanna in 1892, because we had not passed through Sarabit-el-Kadim.

On March 19th we started, as we thought, at 6.45, and walked for two hours down a long sandy slope called the Dababat, then rode over another dreary waste, interspersed with limestone rocks to Wady Tahbus and Wady Bada', where we descried in the dim distance the blue mountains of Jebel Attaka in Africa. At 11.30 we were glad to rest under some rocks two hours before reaching the beautiful cliffs with the Sinaitic inscriptions, under whose broad shadow we had lunched in 1892 and 1893. Our sheikh said that it was four hours from this spot to Sarbout-el-Jamal, and we said it was two-and-a-half. We rode from 2.30 till 5.30, passing Sarbout-el-Jamal, then walked down Wady Hamr (whose mouth is called Shebeikeh), and at seven o'clock we reached our tents, pitched on a spot which Hanna had selected in 1892, and where they would have been in 1893 had my orders been followed instead of the sheikh's, in a kind of recess not far from the mouth of Wady Hamr. A big black flying beetle, called *dabur*, startled us by falling on the table after dinner; and the full moon rose in great glory behind Sarbout-el-Jamal five times her usual size.

Starting next morning before seven we walked for two hours to the spot where we had encamped in 1893. We lunched beneath the palms trees of Wady Useit. The camels were sniffing the air and looking upwards, so the Bedawîn expected the rain, which they really believed had been kept back by our work among the Convent MSS! We talked with them about the education of their children, and one of them said that they had once asked the monks to open a school at Sinai, but they were told that the children could not be received in the garden, and that they themselves shifted about so much as to make it impossible for a teacher to follow them. Some amusing stories were being told, and I felt inclined to contribute the tale of the clergyman who was preaching to a congregation of farmers, and who waxed eloquent on the parable of the Prodigal Son, saying "I should not wonder if the father had kept that calf, fattening it up for years." I was checked however by the thought that Joseph alone amongst my audience had ever heard the story of the Prodigal Son, and as our camel drivers all said they could not read, I resolved to let them hear the story itself. A Bedawy was despatched to the top of Hammam Fara'on to bring me some of the boiling hot sulphur water for a foot-bath. Heavy rain fell most of the night as we slept at Ghurundel. In the morning the little trees looked refreshed, but the sand was as dry as ever. Our first care after breakfast was to take our duck, which had been so persecuted by the hens at Sinai, down to one of the pools, where it was very amusing to see her diving and combing her feathers with her webbed feet. I photographed the Jebaliyeh sheikh and some of our camel drivers, and they offered me coffee in return. I approached them again in the afternoon, as they were sitting in a circle, and asked if they would like to hear a story from the *Angeel* (Gospel); they were delighted, and made me sit on some camel furniture. I began by saying that the story was one told by our Lord Jesus Christ to show that Allah is the Merciful, the Compassionate. They listened with open mouths whilst I read Luke xv, and the tears were rolling down more than one face. I then asked if they had understood it all, and they replied "about the half." So I shut the book and told it once again, leaving out the longer words, they repeating almost every sentence after me. I had a difficulty in pronouncing *'igl* ("calf"), so one of them suggested that I should substitute for it *charûf* ("sheep or lamb.") There are no calves in the Sinai peninsula, so it was an apt illustration of the way in which folk-tales are altered when they are carried to various climes. I then said that there was a passage in the story of St. Paul which I wanted them to know, but as it was a fine piece of eloquence to which a foreigner like myself could not do justice, I hoped they would not object to hearing it from Joseph. Immediately there were cries of "Joseph! Joseph!" and the young man had to rise from his midday siesta to ask why he was wanted. Matters being explained to him he took his seat on the camel-saddle, remarking, "The Prophet says in the Qurân that it is good for us to know both the Torah and the Angeel." He then read St. Paul's speech at Athens very slowly and deliberately, the Bedawîn exclaiming "*Taîb, Taîb*" ("good, good") at the end of every sentence, especially when they heard that "God dwelleth not in temples made with hands," and "hath made of one blood all nations of the earth." It seemed to me that these teachings come more heartily from the lips of Evangelical Protestants than from those of any other Christians, for though our Greek and Romanist friends would doubtless say that God is to be found outside their beautiful churches as well as inside, yet the Moslems cannot be expected to comprehend any subtle distinction, and those who do not rely upon visible accessories to spiritual worship will naturally find a readier acceptance with these idol and image-hating people. The poor men looked so wistfully at us that I felt sure they must be conscious of there being something in the world which they have not got, and the lack of which places them in a position of hopeless inferiority to Europeans. I have been unable to find any trace of missionary work having been done amongst the natives of the Sinai penin-sula of late years, though I should only be too glad to know that in this I am mistaken. We finished our conference that afternoon by accepting a cup of delicious coffee, and an enthusiastic vote of thanks was passed to me and Joseph.

After a night of heavy rain we walked to 'Ain Howarah and photographed it; then mounting our camels we got on the line of some still wireless telegraph poles which had just been put up betwixt 'Uyûn Musa and Tor, and I asked the Bedawîn how they would like to see a railway taking people from Suez to Sinai in five hours. To my great surprise they exclaimed, "Oh, we would be so glad! we would help to make it and help to work it!" They probably did not know what they were speaking about, for they have no power of work in their arms, and none of the methodical habits which are so essential to the safety and comfort of travellers. Orientals are very apt to imagine by adopting the mechanical advantages which they see Europeans enjoying, they will obtain an equal degree of power and influence, whereas these advantages are but the outward expression of the well-trained energy and altruism which has been fostered by Christianity. I do not forget the great advances in civilization which were made by the nations of antiquity before our Lord's advent, but it is a curious fact that the study of nature in a scien-tific way, and the consequent harnessing of her mighty forces to the service of man, has been pursued only within the confines of Christendom.

We lunched somewhere beyond Wady Amarah, and started

again at 2.30. A cold wind blew all day, and at 4.30 we were caught in a flying column of sand. We rode against it for fifteen minutes, holding our broad-rimmed pith hats, when my sister lost control of her parasol and called out to the men to stand still. They paid no attention, for the wind drowned her voice, and I therefore shouted also, with the result that Joseph jumped down and ran to my help instead of my sister's. Looking round, I saw her camel kneeling and in the act of rising again, while her clothes were flapping and her belongings flying in all directions, the sand beating so violently against us as to make us all distracted. Joseph flew to her side, and I thought it better to dismount and comfort her as I best could. Even with my veil down, the sand filled my eyes and mouth. We walked against the wind for half-an-hour, keeping on our feet with no little difficulty, then re-mounted, and in a few minutes we saw the old Jebaliyah sheikh and another man who were riding before us turn suddenly to the right. We followed them, and found our tents pitched in the feeble shelter of a small sand hillock, the bed-room tent held by four extra ropes. We dined in it though its canvas was flapping like a shirt hung out on a clothes-line in a hurricane.

We had a very stormy night and some heavy showers, so sleep came only in snatches and by reason of great weariness. We scrambled through our breakfast in some fashion, and started as we thought at 6.30, wondering why the sun seemed to rise later than he had done at the same season in bygone years. We walked to the strip of little bushes in Wady Samûr; it took us forty minutes to ride across it, the wind blowing so hard that I thought it would drive me off my camel. It was all I could do to keep on cloak and hat. Then came a hail storm, the stones striking both the camels and ourselves like little pebbles. It was followed by very cold rain. Sand, hail, and rain alternated with each other every few minutes, and we were continually mounting and dis-mounting as our confidence ebbed and waned. Heavy clouds were coming up from the sea, and the pitiless blast swept over the great sandy plain, so that at noon we could have imagined ourselves more readily to be on a Scottish moorland in winter than in the Arabian desert. We decided not to pitch our luncheon tent, but to sit for half-an-hour on some stones at the foot of a telegraph pole and discuss a few eggs, biscuits, and dates. At 12.30 we continued our journey, and in half-an-hour we reached the little sand hills that fringe this great tiresome plain on the northern side. After a battle of nearly four hours more with blowing and pelting hail and cold rain we came in sight of 'Uyûn Musa, and dismounted. As we walked my handkerchief was blown out of my pocket and carried off, dancing like a feather in the wind. Joseph ran after it, but as he came near it was tossed aloft, and fled behind a distant hill away to the illimitable desert. Ibrahim, with the sheikh and baggage camels were only a few minutes behind us, and a Bedawy, darting out of the caravan, pursued the white flying thing, and brought it to me in triumph. His fleetness made us think of how the Bedawy prophet Elijah ran before Ahab's chariot like a *sais* from Carmel to the entrance of Jezreel (I Kings xviii. 46).

One of the two fenced gardens at 'Uyûn Musa has been divided into two little ones, in one of which the *wakeel's* house still stands, and another large new garden has been planted beyond them, thus making four gardens instead of two. One of them contains a small whitewashed house with green Venetian shutters, built as the summer quarters of the Syrian shopkeeper in Suez. Though unoccupied most of the year, its brand-new appearance takes something away from the primitive character of the place. We sought in vain for the hostel and stable which have been described by a recent traveller. No animal has ever been used in these gardens for any purpose, the largest well being worked by a *shadoof*. We asked the Bedawîn if there had ever been a stable, and they exclaimed: "What for? for our camels? Their stable is the sand." The principal change in this district is the large new quarantine station nearly two miles distant on the shore. It has been rendered necessary by the outbreak of the plague at Bombay, and at this season it was deserted; but when it is occupied no communication is permitted between its inhabitants and those of the oasis. It is very fortunate that so lonely a spot exists so near the Asiatic end of the Suez Canal.

The storm continued to rage all night, the rain being so heavy that the sand actually became wet. Our tent ropes were fastened to the palm trees, and these also sheltered us from the blast, so we could sleep in peace.

It was a different matter for the little felucca, in which we embarked next day, to make her way up the creek to Suez, and more than once a wave broke over my knees as I sat in it. Port Tewfik was unapproachable in a sailing craft. The Bedawîn made several jokes about their camels being a more comfortable means of progression. On reaching the hotel we discovered why the sun had appeared to rise so late. All our watches were an hour fast, for we had set them wrong by the watch of a young German traveller who had visited the Convent. We had therefore been rising at 4.30 and starting at six.

In the afternoon we distributed the usual backsheesh to our escort in the hotel verandah—four shillings each to eleven of them, and they were evidently satisfied, for they shook hands with us and invoked blessings on our heads. We felt very sorry for these poor men, who had never slept beneath a roof all their lives, and in whose wistful eyes we could read a longing to know something beyond the desert.

The literary results of our journey are still passing through the press, but one permanent effect remains in the strength and power of locomotion which it helped me to regain. My doctor did not mean it altogether as a jest when he said that he would henceforth send all his rheumatic patients to Sinai. I cannot think that he would advise them to undergo the toil and risks of a land journey, but perhaps the day may come when some enterprising person will start a little sanatorium in the Wady Hebrân, where the pools of clear pure water gleam beneath a sapphire sky amongst the bare majestic mountains, and will make a road practicable for light conveyances across the plain from Tor, with Sinai as the chief item in its programme of excursions, and thus make a winter paradise for the victims of our island fogs and drizzles.

CHAPTER IX

ANOTHER "SAYING OF JESUS"

IN CONCLUDING the narrative of our last visit to Sinai, I have to record that the work done by Mrs. Gibson and me on the Palestinian Syriac Lectionaries in the Convent of St. Catharine has brought to light a very remarkable variant in one of our Lord's discourses. It is found only in the manuscript discovered by Dr. Rendel Harris,★ and its full significance was first pointed out by Dr. Nestle.

Whilst the other two extant copies of the same Lectionary, *i.e.* the one in the Vatican and the one found at Sinai by myself, contain the reading of Matt. xii, 36, which is common to all Greek MSS, viz.:

"But I say unto you, that every idle word which men shall speak they shall give account thereof in the day of judgment,"

this one has—

"But I say unto you, that every good word which men shall not speak, they shall give account thereof in the day of judgment."

★ See p. 173.

When we remember the concluding words of St. John's Gospel, "There are also many other things which Jesus did, the which, if they should be written every one, I suppose that even the world itself could not contain the books that should be written," we can have no difficulty in supposing that a saying, or the half of a saying, which fell from His lips, and yet failed to find a place in the authenticated record, might yet linger in the memory of some disciple, find its way into an early copy of the Gospel, and come down to us even through some obscure channel.

True, Codex C. of the Palestinian Syriac Lectionary cannot, like the Logia of Messrs. Grenfell and Hunt, lay claim to the prestige of great antiquity, for it bears a date equivalent to A.D. 1118. But it is evidently copied from an earlier manuscript, quite independently of the other two Palestinian Syriac Codices; and its reading of Matt. xii, 36 has two witnesses to its genuineness, one being in itself, the other in its context.

If we agree with Dr. Rendel Harris that it is the dropped half of a Logion, whose full text would be—

"But I say unto you, that every idle word that men shall speak, and every good word that men shall not speak, they shall give account thereof in the day of judgment,"

we shall find its sequence very appropriate—

"For by thy words thou shalt be justified, and by thy words thou shalt be condemned."

The witness of this text to itself is indeed so striking that every scholar and every thoughtful man or woman to whom we have told it considers it important. When a phantom of the Virgin Mary appeared to Bernadette at Lourdes, or when the ghosts of our departed friends rap on a table, the greater part of what they utter is twaddle. Even the sayings attributed to our Lord and to His blessed Mother in early apocryphal writings fall far beneath the simple dignity of those recorded by St. Paul and by the four Evangelists. Yet this one, attested as it is by a single late manuscript, has an application so searching, an application which touches so nearly the springs of our life and conduct, that we do not feel as if it were sacrilege to attribute it to Him to spake as never man spake.

I do not wish to close my book with a sermon, not even with one from a text so fresh as this; but I should like to draw attention to its more obvious corollaries. It tells us how unwise we may sometimes be when we check our own generous impulses by considerations of worldly prudence, or by the fear of consequences. It surely suggests something to those people who regard all strangers with what the late Poet Laureate has so aptly called "a stony British stare," and to those who designedly pass their friends in the street without a sign of recognition; to those politicians and newspaper-writers also who never try to quench the flames of warlike passion. And it suggests that the highest Christian ideal is not that of a passive abstention from evil, but is one of active kindness to our fellow men.

No more precious lesson than this has been found under the shadow of Sinai. But the value which we can give to its authority as a "saying of Jesus" must be determined by abler pens than mine.

Open to Epiphanies
An Anthology of Commentary, Verse and Aphorism
VYVYAN AURET PRITCHARD

Open to Epiphanies is a beautifully designed Anthology of commentary, essay, verse and aphorism. Three major themes are adopted – Secrets to be Shared, The Search for Values, and The Mysterious and the Infinite. Subjects touched upon include: Déjà Vu, Ethical Responsibility, Grace, Humility, the Social Revolution, and Testimony of Love. Collected from a wide variety of sources, this insightful book embraces many religions and spiritual movements – Buddhism, Christianity, Hinduism, Judaism, Sikhism, Jainism, the Tao, Zen – and provides a wonderful introduction to all who seek the magic of an eclectic Anthology.

Paperback ISBN 1 898595 13 5   £14.95 $24.95
To be published in 2003

The Holy Spirit: Divine Witness Within
VYVYAN AURET PRITCHARD

The truth of the Holy Spirit – so essential to Christian life and service – is wrapped up in mystery. This books sets out to unravel that mystery and explains in straightforward language the major issues that pertain to the Holy Spirit: its personality, its convicting power, its regenerating grace.
Paperback ISBN 1 898595 32 1   £12.95 $19.95

A companion volume to the above book, *The Holy Spirit: Matrix of Destiny and Redemption*, will be published in 2004.
Paperback ISBN 1 898595 38 0   £12.95 $19.95

The Glass of Time
BISHOP BULLEY DD

"Rare is the man who would dare to claim, in this century of doubt and strife, that his trust has never faltered! Happy is the man who though he stumbles reaches ever and again for the outstretched hand of God! . . . But how? I cannot answer for another, but for myself – by staying my eye on God, in meditation, in corporate worship, through ties or sacrament and prayer. I know of no other way – but I know that for me and countless millions these ways suffice."

Paperback ISBN 1 898595 06 2 £12.95 $24.95

The Bible as Theatre
SHIMON LEVY

Although the Old Testament has been thoroughly analysed as literature, and many of its highly dramatic chapters, stories, poetry and prophecies have been adapted for theatre, the Bible *as* Theatre has hardly been dealt with.

A close reading of the OT exposes a refined sense of theatricality, in the usage of space, lighting, costumes and props. God, in theatrical terms, is The Great Offstage Being, in whose name and for whose glory the action is performed.

Paperback ISBN 1 898723 51 6 £15.95 $24.95

The Doctrine of the Trinity: God in Three Persons
MARTIN DOWNES

Paperback ISBN 1 902210 05 0 £13.95 $24.95

Gnosticism: Beliefs and Practices
JOHN GLYNDWR HARRIS

Paperback ISBN 1 902210 07 7 £13.95 $24.95

Christian Theology: The Spiritual Tradition
JOHN GLYNDWR HARRIS

"Dr Harris brings to his task a long and rich career in theology
and education. There is immense learning and great erudition.
A welcome introduction to the heart of Christian believing."
Paul Ballard, Cardiff University
"It is inviting to read, accessible and lucid in its exploration of
the basic concepts of both theology and spirituality." *Professor
Dr. D. Byron Evans D.Litt.,* DD

Paperback ISBN 1 902210 22 0 £14.95 $24.95

Real Prayer Explained
VYVYAN AURET PRITCHARD

"Prayer is the divinest exercise the heart of man can
engage in." *William Law*

Paperback ISBN 1 898595 39 9
To be published in 2003